A 100 Mile Journey

Plus a Few Extra

A Pacific Crest Trail Adventure

L. Michele Scott

ISBN: 9798584090364
Copyright © 2020 L. Michele Scott
All rights reserved.

*This novel is dedicated
To Richard Scott Sr.
Rest in peace, pop*

Published by L. Michele Scott
Follow on Twitter @L_Michele_Scott
Follow on Instagram @geeky_girl_adventures

GeekyGirl.Adventures@gmail.com

This book is not a work of fiction. All rights reserved. No portion of this book may be reproduced mechanically, electronically, or by any other means including photocopying without the written consent of the publisher and author.

PCT Journal
Chapter One
Pre-Hike

November 2018

Things have gotten very REAL over the last couple of weeks, especially this past Wednesday, November 14th. What's so important about a date, in the middle of the week, months before starting a thru-hike of the Pacific Crest Trail? It is Permit Day.

Back when I'd first heard of the trail in 2013, the need to obtain a permit to thru-hike didn't exist. Well, you *did* need permits for certain wilderness areas, etc. – and a permit from the Pacific Crest Trail Association covered most, if not all of these. Over the past couple of years, in an attempt to lessen the impact of the droves of hikers sauntering on the trail, the Pacific Crest Trail Association (PCTA) began implementing a "50 permits a day policy" for North-bounders. I thought this was a great idea to prevent a ton of hikers hitting the same towns and trail angels all at the same time and straining resources, until I was unlucky and missed my target start date for permit day. Heck, not even *close* to my desired date in the beginning of April.

I did manage to book a date three weeks before, during the middle of frosty March. I'm trying to console myself with the fact that sometimes March can be warm and not freezing overnight down here. I live in a desert area of Southern California and I am familiar with the extremes in the weather, and honestly that month can swing either way. More than likely, it will be cold. After a few days of teeth gnashing about my start date, I decided that it's not all that bad – after all, I do better in the cold than in hot conditions while hiking. However, my worry is that I'll reach the Sierra far too early to safely enter given my non-technical hiking skill set for snow. What's a girl to do?

In the meantime, I'm logging in to the permit page online a few times each day, hoping that someone cancels and frees up a spot closer to my desired date in early April. If not…well, I can always take time off trail when close to home and go back to work for a few weeks before starting out again. Not an ideal situation, but at least it is workable.

Also, I continue to watch 2018 vloggers on YouTube, those that are still in the process of posting videos, while tweaking my gear for this spring and mentally preparing for the journey.

***

You may be asking, "What is a thru-hike?"

There are many arguments over what consists of a real 'thru-hike'. The easiest way to explain it is a 'thru' is a continuous footpath between the southern and northern terminus of a trail. Some hikers walk it north to south, some south to north, and others flip flop and hike all its miles out of order. Any of these three are considered thru-hiking.

***

My need to hike the Pacific Crest Trail had nothing to do with escaping from everyday life. I love my family and friends and like my job. I don't believe I am suffering from a midlife crisis (although I *am* the correct age for this to happen) or trying to work through problems while on trail, nor did I feel like I needed to prove something by hiking all of it. Honestly, I don't think I entirely *know* why I want to hike the entire trail. It's just something I feel compelled to do.

How did I hear about the trail? I've lived in Southern California my entire life, but never had heard about the Pacific Crest Trail (PCT) until 2013 when I started hiking around the desert within driving distance of home.

Being the gaming and technology geek that I am, in 2012 I was introduced to the hobby of geocaching. The best way to describe it is using "Multi-million-dollar satellites to find Tupperware in the woods". You laugh, but it's true! There are urban hides as well, but the larger 'caches' are planted along or near hiking trails in larger containers for geocachers to trade items as well as sign the log inside. I found the geocaches out in nature a lot more fun to go and try to find than urban hides, and so I started hiking to find them. I went deeper and deeper along trails to nab the next hidden cache. Eventually, I discovered a small Meetup group online based out of Redlands, California, that wanted to do 4 miles along the PCT near Cabazon because there were a series of caches hidden along it. This was a really easy way to grab multiple numbers during one good hike. One of the guys that came to that hike had thru-hiked the Appalachian Trail and more recently the PCT. He told the rest of us all about the trail; where it went, how long it was, how stinky "hiker trash" hiked all the miles for the joy of successfully completing the trail and calling themselves a thru-hiker.

I was hooked. Seriously hooked. I didn't know anything like this existed, let alone ran border to border along the entire western United States. I'm a bit mortified as I don't remember this guy's name, but he is responsible for creating the spark which fueled my obsession for the PCT. Immediately after returning home from the hike, I fired up my computer, logged into my Amazon account and bought several books and guides on the trail. I had loads of delicious reading in my future. Believe it or not, I'd never even heard of the infamous *Wild* until after I first set foot on the trail. *Wild* was initially a best-selling book by Cheryl Strayed and later a movie starring Reese Witherspoon. Although the author did not hike the Pacific Crest Trail in its entirety, she brought a lot of attention to the trail.

The desert where I live contains many miles of hiking trails, and I began to explore them…and hunt geocaches. Special days were reserved for when I could set foot on the PCT again. On maps I saw that the trail crossed Highway 74 on the way up the mountains into Idyllwild, about a mile from the Paradise Valley Café where Highways 371 and 74 crossed. Picking a day in late spring, I decided to drive up, park my car in the dirt trailhead parking lot, and hike 3 or 4 miles in for a nice 6 to 8 mile 'out-and-back' hike.

It was a hot day, and other than a few day hikers, I saw no one else for quite a while. This was also my first experience peeing in nature while hiking. Answering 'line one' of the call of nature is one of my least favorite things about hiking… not *the* worst, but close. I'm sure you can guess what *is* the most horrible thing. 'Line two'.

I noted some areas that were big enough to pitch a small tent here and there. Nothing established, but you could tell someone had camped there in the past.

Eventually, I saw a hiker heading south along the trail toward me. As he came closer, I noted a large pack, a salt-stained shirt, and a beat-up Tilley hat upon his head with patches on it. We both said our hellos as he hiked by, then I noticed the patches were mile numbers among other things. My excitement rose as I realized this guy was not just a day hiker!

"Hey!" I began enthusiastically. "Are you a thru-hiker?"

He stopped and smiled, turning back to me with a tired, "Yeah."

In the presence of a rock star, I asked, "South bound?!"

As he nodded, I did some internal calculations. It was May. If he was a SoBo (southbound) hiker, he started in Washington in a crazy time of year to begin a southbound hike of the PCT.

I asked him what month he started. He said February. February! In the Pacific Northwest? Holy crap!

This was in 2013 as well, looking back at snowpack graphs it was a low snow year, but regardless, starting at that month meant trudging through the Sierra in early April.

I asked him how he dealt with the snow. He mentioned crampons or microspikes. It's been awhile, so I'm unsure as to which he said he actually used for his hike. Before we parted ways, he asked how long it was to Highway 74 and the Paradise Valley Café. I wasn't too far from the trailhead at that point, a bit over a mile. I told him how far from the 74 it was and that when he reached the top of the next hill, that he would be able to see the café off to the right in the distance. Relief spread across his face and we both continued on our separate ways.

I hiked onward for another couple of miles into a boulder-strewn area where the trail climbs in elevation. (As I write this in 2019, the PCTA announced that this part of the trail would finally be reopened from the fire that hit later that season in 2013. I'm curious to see how it's changed and very glad not to have to take detours around the area during my thru-hike attempt.)

After the hike that day, I had planned to visit the Paradise Valley Café that sits a mile from the Highway 74 PCT trailhead and ask questions from the servers and owner about hikers and the trail. Now, on my way back to where I parked my car, I also hoped to catch the southbound hiker and pick up his tab if it wasn't too late. Why? I'm not sure. I just felt that if someone plodding *that* long, in crazy conditions lived to tell about it, they deserved a break. The only way I could help was to buy him a free lunch. Secretly, I think I was also hoping he would take the time to talk about the trail with me. (Spoiler alert! He did!)

With the right gear, and enough experience, he was successful in making it down to where I met him. For those of you following along using Halfmile (or the National Geographic) maps, the Paradise Valley Café is in Section B of California…a mile west of PCT mile 151.9.

I had hoped to keep in touch with him, and had him jot down his Facebook username, but the writing was so shaky, I couldn't decipher it later. I have no clue who this hiking superstar was to this day, only that he had hiked the Appalachian Trail as proven by patches he wore on his Tilley hat. Now he was close to conquering the Pacific Crest Trail.

Now I *knew* that I would have to try to thru-hike this trail. Every person I met that has thru-hiked it, or even completed a long section hike, fueled my rabidness for the trail. Fast forward a few years later and I finally make the decision to attempt my northbound (NoBo) thru-hike in 2019 when I will be 50 years of age for most, if not all, of the trip. (I will turn 51 in September.) What better way to celebrate being on this earth for half a century? There's also the fear that I'm not getting any younger, and if my parents are any hint to my mobility in 25 plus years, I better do it *now* and not later 'after I retire'. (If I ever can retire... I have a feeling I'll be working until the day I drop.)

That decision was made a couple of years ago. Since then I have been researching, gathering and testing gear, saving money, binge watching hundreds of vlogs of hikers on the trail, studying Yogi's guide, and making pace and hour adjustments on Craig's PCT Planner. I can't tell you how many times I've changed or rearranged where I was going to stop along the way or how I was going to resupply.

Did I mention that I am an over planner? Oh yeah. Big time.

***

My loved ones and friends are very glad that I'm finally attempting the thru-hike as I have driven them crazy talking about the PCT every chance I get over the last few years. In fact, my partner Tami, has told me in no uncertain terms that I'm not allowed to come home until I finish the trail!

***

February 2019

The second permit day has come and gone, and I was able to nab my desired April 7th start date. I'm ecstatic! Now the weather will be warmer, unless a late spring storm rolls through to keep us hikers on our toes.

One benefit to starting in April is that I can now stay at the legendary Scout and Frodo's house the night before my step off date. They are retiring from 'trail angeling' after 2020, so I count myself as one of the lucky ones. Scout and Frodo hiked the trail together in 2007 and have hosted hikers in their homes in San Diego since 2006. From those that vlogged their journey and started at their home, I know that they have several large tents set up in their backyard for hikers, provide dinner and breakfast, as well as giving rides to the southern terminus of the trail an hour or so away. Of course, they cannot all do this by themselves with the large number of hikers that stay with them. They also have a small army of volunteers that help.

In July 2017, I started a YouTube vlog to document the hike in 2019. Seems early to do that, but as I write this, I find the last year and a half has flown by. I wanted to figure out how to vlog, edit and upload while giving myself an abundance of time to do it. The channel is dedicated to the experience of my PCT hike, but also the prep work I did leading up to it (among other, non-hiking, hobbies). I want to document everything. I also hope to give back to the PCT vlogger community as I learned *so* much from those that came before me by watching their videos about the trail…

and about gear, gear, gear. I plan on taking video and pictures primarily with my cell phone. It can take surprisingly high-quality photos! When I compared it to my GoPro 5, the quality was about the same. I do plan to bring my GoPro along as well for a backup and to take night sky shots if possible.

Every weekend I'm on fun hikes to practice for the thru-hike and recording most of it with my phone. I had one particular failure on an overnight trip to the White Water preserve with fellow PCT 2019 hopefuls Patty and Maru. After a short hike, we set up our tents in the preserve only to have the sky open up on us and dump an insane amount of rain. It can also get very cold at the preserve and all of us bailed at some point during the night because of freezing rain and wetness inside our tents. The rain was pelting down so hard; I literally dragged my tent and gear across the grass, closer to my car and chucked everything in haphazardly before running back across the campground to say goodbye to the others. When I arrived home late that night, I spread everything out in the garage and let it dry over the next few days. The oddest thing was, I had torn a small hole in the bottom of my tent, yet its protective footprint was unscathed. How did that happen?

No worries. I patched the hole later. Good as new!

***

March 2019

I'm seeing some early starters begin the trail via comments and photos on social media as well as videos posted with creative names. So, I decided to rebrand my YouTube channel from my boring ol' name to something memorable and self-descriptive. I still have a while to go until I start, but the excitement is rising! With the excitement is the battle of not losing focus in everyday life. Work is difficult because all I can think about is getting on the PCT. My training hikes are even tough because I'm completely 'over' the training hikes and want to be on the actual trail. In a way, I'm regretting not starting in March near the start dates of many of my friends, but still feel as if it would be too early and too cold weather-wise for me and the snow conditions that they will likely hit around San Jacinto and Baden Powell. Snow is still around and there's always the risk of a late spring storm bringing more.

Speaking of snow, the fear mongering about the Sierra snowpack started even before many of us set foot on the trail. Throughout the winter, many of us who live in California kept saying, "Well, yes there's a lot of snow. It's *winter*!"

Now, as spring approaches, the official reports are comparing this year to 2017, a high snow year in the Sierra. Well OK. It *is* more than just the regular snow we get in winter before the spring and summer thaw. Urgh, this is going to be an interesting and scary hike. One of my fears of hiking the PCT is the Sierra in a high snow year. No snow skills here, even though I have practiced a couple times with an ice axe and microspikes in our local mountains. I should not get into the Sierra until around June 1st, but even then, with these conditions…

Hoping for a dry spring in the Sierra and thaw to hit early, but not too hot, the river crossings are going to be insane – rapid and a potentially high level of water. I'm tall, just shy of six feet, and can use that height as an advantage on crossings, but I'd rather not be too challenged by them.

***

In the week leading up to Tami dropping me off at Scout and Frodo's, I worked at my job during the day and by night started checking off a list I made for items needed for the hike as I packed them inside my backpack. I want to make sure I don't forget anything crucial to the thru-hike. While stuffing everything inside, I am amazed at the amount of gear that can fit in the ULA pack. A year ago, when my base weight was over 18 lbs., I purchased the Catalyst model instead of the more thru-hiker popular Circuit. The Catalyst was rated for over 18 lbs. Now, a year later, I managed to shave my base weight down to 16.5 lbs. but kept the larger volume pack. I really enjoy that pack – it's sturdy for such a lightweight bag.

Chapter Two
It Begins

April 6th, 2019

    Tami convinced a friend of hers to come along for the ride to San Diego and all three of us set out early in the day. We stopped at the Paradise Valley Café for some brunch. This is the same café I ate at with the southbound hiker years before, the one where the Pacific Crest Trail crosses Highway 74 in our local mountains. I spied some potential thru-hikers and walked over to say hello. I guess I didn't look, or quite smell the part of a true hiker yet, as they were a little stand-offish. Oh well.
    Soon. I thought. *Soon.*
    On the way to San Diego my phone 'dinged'. I pulled it from the side pocket of my hiking shorts and brought up a message from one of my friends who had already begun the trail days, even weeks before. In it was a photo of three couples, all smiling and relaxing by a picnic table in Warner Springs at mile 110. Patty & Maru from Southern California, Corey & Chelsea from Oregon, and Heidi & Brian from Liverpool, England. All three were fast friends from social media. A feeling of disappointment overcame me as I wanted to hang out with them and perhaps hike alongside. For a few moments I considered asking Tami to take the turn and drive

to Warner Springs instead of continuing on to San Diego. However, I didn't want to get in to Scout and Frodo's too late if I could help it, so we kept moving toward San Diego.
Maybe I can catch at least one couple, I thought. Maybe.

The drive was long, but we reached Scout and Frodo's place a bit after 3PM. They give orientation tours, but I was too early for the next one. Instead, I wandered around with Tami, looking at the well-organized set up our hosts had created with the help of many volunteers. Their garage is dedicated to mailing packages and has a large sink for brushing teeth and washing hands. They have two restrooms in the house for hikers to use, but sometimes host thirty hikers a night, so time is precious and the large sink in the garage can cut time spent in the other rooms to a minimum. The kitchen bustled with activity, volunteers cooking dinner for us hikers for later that evening. The first trail register sat on a long dining table that was covered with a large, white tablecloth. It wasn't the register that grabbed my attention right away, but the tablecloth itself. On it was drawn (or printed) a full map of the Pacific Crest Trail as it wound its way through California, Oregon and Washington. It was amazing!

Outside, the backyard overflowed with several large tents, spread out on bright green, artificial turf except for one corner of the yard where many chairs set in a large circle. A modest sized tree house perched above the tents in one corner of the property for hikers to camp in.

After a tearful goodbye…
OK not a tearful goodbye…let's try that again.
I almost cried when Tami left, but I held those feelings back because I did not want her to leave sad, or worse, annoyed that I was blubbering even though I was finally beginning my dream of hiking the PCT. I expected to

be home in a couple of weeks for a double zero if I could keep the pace I thought I was capable of maintaining between the town of Campo and the Paradise Valley Café area.

So, after an almost tearful goodbye, I walked back to the lime-green tent I chose to stay in and started unpacking my backpack until it was time for orientation. Frodo had pointed out that signs on each tent that told you how many people they could hold. Mine said three, but I saw that would be a snug fit.

One girl from a nearby tent came by and asked if she could move into this tent as she was not leaving the following morning and everyone else in the tent she was sleeping in were due to leave tomorrow. She was from out of the country – Scout and Frodo allow international hikers to stay more than one night.

I said, "Sure you can stay here, but I'm packing up tomorrow morning too. I'll try to be quiet, so I don't bug ya."

She was all right with just me packing up rather than four or five other hikers in the other tent and moved in. Her name was Seraina – and no, I don't know if that's the correct spelling or even if I have the name completely right, but she is Seraina to me! It sounded similar to 'Sarina'. (I'm not sure if she will ever read this, but if so, please correct me if I'm terribly off with your name.)

Another international hiker named Arthur approached me as I was exploding my backpack in the tent, organizing my gear. He introduced himself and told me that he recognized me from my vlogs on YouTube. I was surprised as I don't have many followers but found out he is a friend of Freddy from the Netherlands. Freddy is a 'friend' of mine on Facebook who I virtually talk to on the PCT Class of 2019 page. He started the trail a number of days before and is a strong hiker, with the ability to do many miles early in the hike. I likely will never catch him, but I think Arthur plans to do so. Arthur is starting tomorrow, along with me, and at least twenty-five other hikers from Scout and Frodo's house.

In the evening, I had "Jiggy", a PCT hiker from a prior year, assist with a pack shake down in an attempt to shave some weight from my pack. Up to that point, I thought I had done a good job keeping my base weight below 18 lbs., but also knew I had thrown a little bit in here and there that may not be needed. With her help, we trimmed about a full pound off my pack weight! Even so, I didn't like the way she had organized items within the pack, so I reorganized it when I got back to the tent where I wouldn't be seen. Nevertheless, thank you for helping me lighten my load, Jiggy. Every ounce counts.

A side note, it turns out that Scout is quite the country music fan, or at least loves to line dance. I've never tried it before, but he talked a number of us onto his lawn and taught us some basic line dancing moves before turning on the music and having us do it live. Oh, yes. We were all perfect in our line dancing form. Really! Ok, maybe not so much, but it was fun. No one was as good as Scout.

These trail angels are amazing and find it in their hearts to do so much for hikers. "Angels" is the correct word to describe them, in every sense of the word. Scout and Frodo will be 'retiring' from hosting after the 2020 season to enjoy their grandkids and rest of true retired life. Somehow, I can't see them removing themselves from PCT 'trail angeling' completely. I would put money down that they will be helping in some form, just not to the degree they currently can.

That evening, we all ate dinner sitting on the lawn chairs and listened to "leave no trace" principles and stories of the trail from Scout, Frodo and friends. At some point after darkness fell, I went back to the green tent and crawled under my quilt. It was hard to fall asleep that night – far too much excitement and anticipation kept my mind active. Tomorrow we plan on being on the road to the southern terminus before dawn.

April 7th, 2019

    Zero dark thirty hit after a hard night of sleep. I was using a new sleeping air mattress that was simply awesome in comparison to what I was trying before, the Big Agnes AXL Insulated. It keeps you off the ground and comfortable, especially if you're a side sleeper. However, it couldn't drown out the noise of people snoring no matter how comfortable you are on it (there is no way to bury your head into the baffles). The tents are awesome, and luckily there ended up only being the two of us in the green, three-person tent, so we weren't climbing over each other during the night for those late night/early morning trips to the restroom. I packed up as quietly as I could, trying not to disturb Seraina. There was a large group of us scheduled to leave that morning for the southern terminus and the start of our PCT adventure – twenty-five alone that were driven from Scout and Frodo's house to the border that morning. The logistics of giving us all rides still amaze me, but they do it. Every year.
    I carried my pack to the front of their house, placed it next to all the other backpacks. The walkway in front of the home was lined with colorful packs, clean… for the last time in a long time. I returned inside for a quick breakfast and last-minute restroom run before the vehicles arrived. All of us were excited and nervous, eating what would be our last non 'trail food' for a day or more unless fast enough to cover twenty miles in the first day and reach Lake Morena.
    It was still dark by the time we piled into different cars in the cool predawn hours. I was in an SUV, driven by 'Carl', which had four other hikers inside besides me. I can't recall everyone's name, but one was using a trail name she had been given on the Appalachian Trail, "Miss Bling" and the hiker sitting directly in front of me was Erick (trail name Dutchman I think). I feel bad. I'm just terrible with names

unless I see you a lot. Although, I never did see Miss Bling again after she started hiking today, she left a 'sparkly' impression. She was wearing glitter and had a bright personality. I can almost envision her spreading fairy dust up the PCT when she began her hike.

A few of us in the SUV had nervous stomachs and convinced Carl to pull off at a convenience store to use the restroom after we discovered that a nearby rest-stop was closed for maintenance. The C-store had one stall. ONE. Needless to say, it took a while before we got back on the road. This may fall under the category of "Too Much Information", but I nearly had an accident by the time we stopped. I'm very grateful our driver pulled over. There's a saying in the thru-hiker world. "You're not a real thru-hiker until you poop your pants" ...or something to that effect. I nearly became an official thru hiker before I touched the southern terminus.

We eventually arrived at the terminus in full daylight to find the other cars of hikers patiently waiting for us. Every day, a photo is taken of all the starters from Scout and Frodo's standing around, and literally on, the terminus monument. After that, everyone will pose and have a selfie taken with it. Mine was not very flattering, but then again, one of my reasons for getting out here is to drop weight. I made sure to sign the register at the monument that every hiker signs and dates before starting (or ending a south bound thru hike). I was nervous again but made sure to walk over to the border fence and peek into Mexico. The fence is currently made of long, corrugated metal, topped with barbed wire, stretching as far as the eye can see. There are holes and small gaps throughout the fence, enough to stick your fingers over the border. I did so to officially 'touch' Mexico before turning around and taking my first proper steps for my thru hike attempt on the PCT.

Author sitting on southern terminus monument of the PCT

The beginning...

The morning was cool as I started, but the forecast was for the mid-80s, so it was not going to remain cool for long. Mile 1 went by quickly, the marker stood hidden around the curve of the trail. I always wondered why the vloggers I watched seemed surprised when they reached it. The sign is suddenly just *there,* and it does surprise you when you walk around the curve and see it. It is also crazy how you round a corner of a hill and it changes from chaparral and scrub brush to tall live oak trees and grass. I just loved shaded areas when I walked through, and sometimes rested, in them.

For example, mile marker 2.7 has a minor running stream with a small wood plank walkway placed over it, and a beautiful, shaded area to rest and camp. Not even a half mile before contained scrub brush and sun exposure. At the stream, a group of German hikers that started in the Scout and Frodo group caught up to me at this point. Arthur was among them. Of course, it was far too soon to even think about camp, but we all stopped here to snack. I took my shoes off and enjoyed airing out my feet in the grass. I was not tired enough for a nap yet, but the cool shade was inviting. As a young child, a field of tall grass lured me into taking a nap when I should have been walking home after school. As an adult, it was still hard to leave this particular patch of heaven. Sighing, I reluctantly squeezed back into my shoes, rolled up the pack and continued onward with the Germans.

By the way, I'm referring to this entire group as being from Germany which may not be entirely accurate. In hindsight, I think a few may have been Dutch or from other Northern European countries.

Approaching mile marker 2.7 – a lush green area

     Almost everyone 'left me in the dust' with their hiking pace except for one couple that was only a little faster than me. We would 'leapfrog' each other every time they took a break or one of us stopped to take photos.

     The last time I saw this particular group of hikers was around mile 3, where the trail crosses train tracks. I'm such a dork. I had to lay down and place my ear on the rail to listen and 'see' if a train was coming. Honestly, who knows if it was even still in service, but the call of childhood enticed me to do it. Didn't hear a thing! We did see two, very large vultures circling overhead though, waiting for one of the original twenty-five hikers to drop on this warm day.

     Glancing around at this point, I was amazed how closely the landscape looked so much like my parents' place in Lake Mathews, California. Tall, rocky hills covered in chaparral and scrub brush with the occasional scraggly tree trying to survive in an arid environment. This year in the desert, the unusual amount of winter rain is resulting in bursts of colors here and there. Wildflowers of all hues are poking up along the trail and on hillsides. I saw lots of poppies today, the state flower of California. I haven't seen that many poppies in years.

Eeek! I also saw my first snake with the couple I was leapfrogging with. It was not a rattlesnake though, thank goodness, but instead a boa. We weren't sure which type of boa it was…a rubber or rosy boa. Seeing it made us all jump, but then we stared fascinated, watching as it crossed the trail, very slowly, for the most part ignoring us humans.

Mile 4.4 – a beautiful creek is here in dappled shade with delightfully cool water. The only downside is poison oak growing near the trail where you cross the small creek. The nefarious plant was pretty easy to recognize so we shimmied by to the other side and found resting spots to eat and filter more water. There was a lot of mica or flecks of gold in the streambed – actually all the little water sources today seemed to have it. And here's me without my gold pan…

Heat was beginning to slow my roll by mile 5. Any sort of strong wind felt delightful by midday. Another mile passed and the heat kept rising while the trail decided to start going exclusively uphill. After mile 6, I thought I better start listening to my body and look for a good campsite even though I was far short of my original goal of 15 and 'backup' plan of 12 miles. The heat, the excitement of day one, and the uphill trend had taken its toll. The path went across a small trickle of water tumbling down, across the trail from above. I did not fill up to capacity there but did refill over a liter of water. I think this may have been a mistake, but I'm so worried about mileage and time.

There's a small campsite around mile 7, but literally only has room for 1 tent…and when I arrived it was already taken by Erick/Dutchman who I had ridden with this morning to the terminus. He was also hurting after a hot day and had his tent nearly up. He is a beast on uphills, but I saw him a few times throughout the day at each water source. I spied an unmarked campsite about a half mile further, but several blossoming ant hills and no shade made me rethink the area and push on. I was worried that I would not find a campsite as no others were marked on Halfmile maps until near mile 12. Guthooks, a phone app with more detailed information on the trail, listed one more between where I stood and mile 12, but I really needed to stop soon. There was no way I could make it all the way to mile 12 based on how I was feeling. I still can't believe I thought I could make it to Hauser Canyon on day one. I've hiked 12 mile days before, but during cooler weather and on milder terrain.

Later, I spied an unmarked seep crossing the trail and thought I should gather more water as the heat had made me drink more than expected. Trudging along the trail to the water, suddenly I heard a loud, angry rattle in the bushes next to a down slope to my right. It's amazing how a quick surge of adrenaline can snap you out of doldrums and force you to react! I snapped to attention and hopped backward a few yards, swearing up a storm. My second snake in one day - on day one! And this one, a rattler! I had to move forward, but there was no way I was going to try to walk by this angry snake, especially as I couldn't see exactly where it was. I only heard it.

Every time I stomped my feet and poles to try to get it to move along, it rattled. I imagined it in the bush, watching me thinking, "Try it bitch. Come get some!"

At an impasse, I continued to stomp around until it finally stopped rattling. Guessing it had finally slithered down the slope enough to not feel threatened by me, I quick stepped it up the trail. I did not stop at the seep – NOPE!

The heat really ramped up by this time and a last-minute luxury item I attached to my pack was proving invaluable this afternoon. Bryan, my partner's son, had given me a scarf with some sort of crystal technology stitched inside. When you immersed it in water (or a lot of sweat), squeezed out excess liquid and 'snapped' it, the scarf became cold and refreshing. At nearly every water source I did this and tied it around my neck, which helped to keep my body temperature down. It was a life saver. Thank you once again Bryan for the gift.

Late that afternoon, I dragged my dead legs to a pipe gate at mile 8.8 and the promise of potential campsites .2 miles further along the trail. I glanced to my left and was ecstatic to see an open flat spot, nestled by some boulders and chaparral – a delightful, and more importantly, completely empty spot to camp. It was a 'dry camp' – which means there's no water nearby and you only have what you hiked in with. My water supply was lower than I felt comfortable with, so I did not cook anything for dinner that needed rehydration. In fact, I didn't have much of an appetite at all, but managed a few hundred calories before settling in to do my chores before bed. This was my first night camping on the PCT and everything was a learning experience. Water was already becoming in issue.

Before calling it a night and curling up under my quilt, I wrote in my journal and edited my first official vlog post. At first, I wasn't going to upload it to YouTube, but had a fantastic signal. I'm always worried about having enough space on my phone for photos and videos, so I uploaded it and hoped my friends and loved ones enjoyed watching. Tomorrow's goal would now be Hauser Canyon, not Lake Morena. The thought of making the steep climb from Hauser Canyon up and over the mountain before Lake Morena in the heat of the afternoon was a deal breaker. Tomorrow was supposed to be a scorcher – far worse than today. This would already make me a day behind schedule. Oh well, people say you need to be flexible on trail.

April 8th, 2019

I tried to get up extra early to avoid the heat, but it was too dark, and my body was craving the extra rest. I waited until the sun came up before eating breakfast and tearing down camp. I slept OK – better than at Scout and Frodo's house, yet was still short on sleep. The camp spot was awesome and, for the most part, quiet. The only thing I heard after nightfall were coyotes howling in the distance. Before nightfall, someone was shooting target practice down in a distant valley.

This may be more "TMI" (Too Much Information), yet I have to point out that the site was a perfect place for the call of nature too. Not too far from where I set up the tent, there are large slabs of rocks and boulders that block the view of the trail and provide a solid surface to lean against. I didn't have any luck though. Hopefully when the call REALLY comes there will be a great location like this again. Hikers on the PCT are encouraged to Leave No Trace whether in camp or hiking. LNT is a practice to minimize our impact on the wilderness and leave it as pristine as possible for all to enjoy. Part of that is packing out ones used toilet paper. Yeah, I know! Gross! Yet, it's worse seeing 'blossoms' of used toilet paper around camping areas and along the trail. Honestly, it turns out to not be as gross or difficult to pack it out as long as you can wrap it up with clean paper and stuff it in a sealable Ziploc used for all your trash.

I smelled something bad as I was packing up this morning and thought that perhaps some of my food was already turning bad in the bag. After sniffing around, I discovered it was *me*, not the food. I heard that hiker 'funk' can be really stinky but didn't expect it so early. People say you become immune and don't smell it after a while. When exactly does that happen? Whew!

Getting a slow start this morning... too slow. The high was forecast to be in the upper 80s and it was important to get an early start. I think I finished packing up and hit the trail around 8 AM. Sounds early, but it's not when you're a thru-hiker and need to walk all day to make miles. It was already uncomfortably warm when I left the campsite.

I saw some proof of the heavy rains this year as I hopped across washed out portions of the trail. Having long legs helped bridge the gaps, but I can only imagine what other parts of the trail must look like. More clues that it's been a 'wet' winter season – I ran across a seep coming down the rocks on the left side of the trail. For the most part, these are not flowing enough to fill up your water bottles. Yet, this one was running enough for me to place my CNOC bladder against the rock wall and gather nearly a half a liter of water to filter. It was also nice and chilled... ahhhh. Here is where I think I made another mistake by not taking the time to gather more water from the seep with the temperatures climbing. I should have collected as much as I could carry.

Not much later, I answered the call of nature and saw a distinct orange color instead of hydrated yellow in my urine. Uh oh. Not cool. At that point, I had a little over a liter of water left on me and still 4 more miles to go to the next water source on the map. Normally it would not have been an issue except it was getting very hot and I was clearly already dehydrated. I was kicking myself at this point. I let others talk me into bringing fewer liters of water than I originally planned. Originally, the plan was to slog 5 liters of water with me... just in case as I know I normally drink a lot of water. Would one extra liter have made life easier or would the extra weight have made me more miserable? Who knows? I *do* know that I was low on water and it was a hot day.

I found myself worrying about Erick/Dutchman who camped behind me at mile 7.4 and hoping he had enough water in this dry stretch. He may have gotten an early start and passed my tent before I was up and about, yet I hadn't heard anyone hike by and no one came around while I packed up.

Focused on making progress and conserving water I was happy when the trail started a short downhill portion. In a few moments I heard rapid footfalls behind me. A trail runner!

Who in the world would be running the trail in this heat? I thought as I moved off to the side to make room.

A guy in a yellow tank top came jogging down the PCT and stops to say hi and ask how I was doing. Then he offers me water! He only has a liter left but swears he doesn't drink much and knows he will be at Hauser creek soon to refill. I didn't let him give me as much as he wanted but did let him top off my last liter. Seriously a life saver!

Before he left, I asked his name.

"Twerk." He said.

The name clicked in my dehydrated mind. "Twerk? As in 'Twerk in the dirt'?"

He said yes, and I turned into a fangirl, gushing about how much I loved his photography before he thanked me and continued down the PCT. For those of you who do not know of him, Twerk has a gift. He took amazing photographs on his thru hike in 2018 and published a coffee table book named, *Hiker Trash Vogue*. This year he is section… running, and also doing Trail Magic up and down the PCT. I didn't see a camera on him but would bet he was continuing to take fabulous pictures of hikers this year as well.

***

Let me interrupt for a moment and define Trail Magic for the uninitiated. It is an unexpected act of kindness left or given to hikers. It can be in the form of water, any sort of food and drink. It also can be as simple as giving rides to town or back to the trail. Some open their homes to hikers! Trail magic renews your love for fellow humans as most are doing it out of the kindness of their hearts. It can be a lot of work for these "Angels" as they are called, but hikers appreciate it more than you can imagine.

***

In a way, Twerk provided my first trail magic experience while hiking *on* the PCT. Technically, Scout and Frodo was my first magic *off* trail.

Not too far after Twerk passed me, another hiker caught me and topped off my liter again. I can't remember his name, but we later started calling him "No Name" when we met up again down at Hauser Creek. Thank you!

Rounding a ridge, I spotted the infamous climb out of Hauser canyon across the ravine. It looks every bit as steep as its reputation. I'm glad I'm waiting to hike it tomorrow morning and not now. It definitely looks like a "wall" that will be tough to conquer.

There's a long dirt road the trail joins right before dropping off into a steep descent to the creek. At this time of day, early afternoon, the sun is completely overhead and is baking me alive. It's a hot and sunny day and I feel sunburnt even after putting on sunscreen. Again, Bryan's cool bandana he gave me helps prevent sunstroke.

Sign before the drop to Hauser creek

Warned ahead of time by other vloggers this season, I did not miss the PCT sign where it veers off the dirt road. Many people do and must slog back up the road to find where the PCT splits away from it. In the heat, exposed as you are, that can't be fun. I thought I could be in cruise control now, only having a little over a mile to the creek, until I realized that most of this mile was rocky, steep descent until you're almost to the water. That last mile took forever, but I made it. Hauser Creek at last! Cool water! (Hauser creek is normally dry, but this season is a wet year and it was flowing strongly.)

I saw Twerk and another hiker named Sage chilling in the shade, drinking water. I unceremoniously dropped my pack, grabbed my CNOC bladder and Sawyer filter and staggered to the creek. Twerk left soon after and No Name sauntered up from behind me to relax and cool off too. I was confused as No Name should be well ahead of me like Twerk was, but apparently missed the turn off and continued down the dirt road for a mile before realizing his mistake. Oops! All three of us sat in the shade for a long time enjoying a rest and chatting. The first to leave was No Name, and Sage kept saying he planned on doing the climb this afternoon in the heat, but later after it cools off. There was no way I was in the condition to try something like this, so I decided to camp literally where I was sitting. I worried about those that kept going this afternoon and hope they all did well.

Hiking in the heat kills appetite. I had ZERO hunger, but after cooling off was able to eat a good-sized meal. I couldn't quite finish it though. It was a double serving of one of my dehydrated meal packs. I sealed it and placed it back in my food bag for later, or breakfast in the morning. My plan is to get up early and leave while the sun hasn't had the chance to start baking us alive.

A couple hours after resting and talking with Sage, who appears at the creek but Erick/Dutchman!

I cheered and said something like, "Yay, you're alive!"

Erick had not passed me after all but knew that water was going to be an issue and hiked BACK south on the PCT to the last water source at mile 6.6ish to fill up before hiking north again to Hauser. He also wanted to take on the climb in the morning and picked a camp spot on the other side of the creek. Sounds like he had as rough of a day as I did but with extra mileage.

A large handful of hikers spread out their tents along the creek that evening. As I wrote in my journal that night, frogs began serenading us to sleep. I love falling asleep to the sound of frogs. The only problem was that Hauser canyon also seems to be on the flight pattern for every helicopter in southern California. Seriously! Immigration, military, etc… you name it, they flew over us.

I'm really looking forward to Lake Morena and a shower tomorrow. I smell like carrion and am being harassed by gnats and flies. Circled by vultures too! I don't smell the other hikers, just me. Although, they say they smell too.

Welcome to the Pacific Crest Trail, sometimes it's your friend, sometimes it feels like your mortal enemy.

April 9th, 2019

I wasn't the first one out of camp, but thankfully for my ego wasn't the last one either. As I mentioned before, there are a good number of hikers camping at the creek last night, lots of company for the climb ahead. I was able to get completely packed up and started to get going by 7:20 AM. Better than the previous day, but still later than I wanted to start.

The climb out of Hauser canyon is no joke. All the stories you hear about it are true. Think of using a Stairmaster at the gym on difficult settings for 3 miles. I can't imagine hiking this in the heat. Morning is the best time, unless you're doing it at night. The trail is completely exposed, but if you're early enough in the morning, there are little pockets of shade here and there to take short breaks. Oh, and when you think you're done with the climb, the trail will slap you right back into reality and remind you that you're *never* done with the uphills.

Looking south while climbing out of Hauser Canyon

A rare green area before Lake Morena

An abandoned backpack was set on the side of the trail along the first mile out of Hauser creek. Well OK, not abandoned. Usually when you come across this, it means that whoever belongs to that pack is off in the bushes taking care of the call of nature. I met the pack owner later as we leapfrogged each other up the trail. His name was Frank from Oregon, one of the few senior aged hikers I had seen on the PCT so far. At one point I passed him while he was having a hiker 'yard sale'. A 'yard sale' is when you find a space to spread out all your damp or wet gear to dry in the sun. Frank had some issues with condensation inside his tent overnight and needed to give his things some time to dry out.

Erick, who I mentioned before, is probably around my age, so nearly a senior or hovering around the half century mark. Maybe he's a decade shy of that mark? I can see him starting below me on the hill taking his first steps of the climb. He's a powerhouse going uphill and I know he will catch and pass me within an hour. He seems to go faster as I fade. I'm doing better than expected on the climb out of Hauser – averaging over one mile an hour. After the initial climb, it rewards you with a nice flat trail and a little downhill then up, up, up once again. Thankfully, it seems to be not as hot today. It is still warm, but even a few degrees cooler makes all the difference in the world. For example, the sun feels like a warm caress rather than flaying the skin from your body with its harsh rays.

I was ever so happy to see my first view of Lake Morena from the ridge high above! There still was a distance to go downhill to the campground that the trail led into, but I could see my salvation from three long hiking days in sight. My first priority when I hit the bottom of the trail was to hunt for the campground restroom with flush toilets and running water. Pure luxury to me now. They were having an E. coli scare at the campground this year, but I still washed away the caked dirt from my hands using soap and water from the sink.

Next priority was food – real food, not trail food. I didn't think that I would be affected like this yet as it's only been three days, but the thought of a cooked meal over rehydrated meals or snack bars quickened my step to the malt shop in town. It was a long road-walk. OK only 1/8th of a mile, but it stretched on forever. Frank, from Oregon, caught up with me and we walked the rest of the way together to have lunch. We put in our order immediately after setting foot in the shop with a busy grill cook and went outside to stake out seats at a table. The smell of other hiker's food made my stomach growl in anticipation. Somehow, I became hungrier – it's not like I was starving mind you. Yet, fresh food is amazing after days of hiking away from civilization. Eventually, my order was ready, and I thought it was one of the most delicious burgers I've ever eaten along with fries and a Powerade. Later, I went back and ordered a chocolate malt. Ahhhh, so much better.

The lady behind the grill was frazzled and overworked trying to feed the locals and the ravenous hikers coming through. If you ever hike the trail, be sure to toss some cash in the tip jar. She works hard to feed us.

As Frank was eating his meal, he sadly decided to end his hike and called Scout (of Scout and Frodo) to come bail him out from the trail. He had underlying health issues and decided hiking the trail with them was not a good idea after all. Bummer! I was sad to see him go but understood and said goodbye after Scout picked him up to take to the airport.

So, I must admit, last night… or actually this morning in the wee early hours while camping next to the creek in Hauser canyon, I thought about trying to find an Airbnb in Lake Morena. The thought of a shower, bed and laundry facilities lured me. I knew that one was nearby since some of my friends, Cory and Chelsea (also from Portland, Oregon), had stayed in one before starting at Campo in mid-March. I know, I know – three days and I'm already 'glamping', but I felt I really needed it at that point. Especially the laundry facilities.

Surprisingly, I had signal down in the canyon and found the ONE home in Lake Morena that rents out rooms via Airbnb. Nearly all the rooms are the same price as renting a cabin at the campground except you have running water at the house, and a real bed. Hmmm, yeah, not a hard choice to make. The map placed the house about a third of a mile from the malt shop too. I requested a room and hoped that I'd have signal again after the climb to see if it was accepted. It was late notice, so there was a chance the owners would turn me down. A little after 8AM and a mile into the climb I saw a response. They accepted my request! I was so happy and really looked forward to a restful stay. There is a chance that the other rooms will be rented – if so, I hope the guests were fellow hikers.

Today is the first time I've felt sore. Really sore. After sitting at the malt shop for lunch, it was hard to get this old body moving again. I shuffled down the road toward the Airbnb house through a quiet neighborhood, keeping my mind on a hot shower and cleaning my stinky hiker clothing. There was no one else there when I checked in, and after a few hours realized that I had the entire house to myself. It was kind of lonely but nice at the same time. I started washing one set of clothing and dried it before I cleaned my sleep layer and took a shower in-between when I had a clean set to put on afterward. That shower was *delightful*... even if it did remind me that I was sunburnt.

The Wi-Fi at the house was very weak, but I just plugged in the phone to power and let it upload a vlog episode over several hours. My vlog channel is growing and gaining subscribers, that's cool! More people watching than just my mom. I hope to continue to do a daily video over the entire hike if my phone storage can hold out.

As I write this day's entry into the journal, I can feel my body sinking into a couch, so exhausted. There's a TV here and I'm just staring at it with glazed eyes, relaxing. I think it's going to be an early night tonight... after getting dinner from the malt shop. Must never pass up the opportunity for fresh food.

Later that evening, I managed to painfully shuffle back to the malt stop and order a pizza for dinner while I picked up a few extra food items to supplement my supply until I reached the next town, Mount Laguna. Not much later, back at the Airbnb house, I didn't last very long after scarfing down a couple pieces of pizza and slept like the dead.

April 10th, 2019

Determined to get an early start this morning, I cleaned, packed up and hit the road by 7:30 AM. I wanted to swing by the malt shop this morning to repurchase some Gatorade packets I had bought the night before. They weren't in my bag later, so figured I perhaps dropped them on the way back or maybe left them at the store. The first thing the cashier said to me as I walked in was if I left two Gatorade packets yesterday at the store. Yup! They actually held on to them for me. I am extremely impressed with the store's honesty.

There are no hikers at the store at this time of day, which is surprising because the breakfast they serve is reported to be excellent here. I had left over pizza from the night before for breakfast and had packed the rest of it out for lunch today too. So, I skipped buying more food here this time around.

I walked down the road and turned right at the campground, skirting along the right side, past the PCT hiker designated spots at the back. The area is known for its wild turkeys, but I didn't see any yesterday or today while hiking out of town. The trail picks up at the edge of the campground and continues a nice, gradual uphill out of Lake Morena. My plan is to make it to the Fred Canyon camp area by the end of today – 12 miles out. It will be my longest day yet if I can do it!

Newer sign vs vintage sign on the PCT past Lake Morena

Let's talk about 'snot rockets'. I'm not sure what it is about hiking, but I find myself constantly congested or having a runny nose. Another hiker, trail name "Night Crawler", made a tongue-in-cheek instructional video last year while hiking the PCT. The video instructed how to correctly take care of a plugged nose while on the trail without using some of your precious toilet paper. Without going into too much detail, I will say that I successfully replicated the method this morning. It sure was wonderful having clear nostrils for a while.

Night Crawler is in the midst of his attempt to thru-hike the Continental Divide Trail this year as I attempt the PCT. If he succeeds, he will complete his 'triple crown'. The triple crown of thru hiking is an earned accomplishment for completing the Appalachian Trail, the Pacific Crest Trail and the Continental Divide Trail. No small feat, to be sure. He also has a vlog channel on YouTube, which is where I discovered him. Fair warning, some people may find him abrasive. I find his candor refreshing – but then again, I'm not one to get excessively upset when around non 'politically correct' people either. I have no plans on attempting a triple crown or even another 'long trail' at this point. My focus is solely on PCT.

There are many yucca plants poking their flowered heads from the surrounding chaparral this morning as I saunter up the trail. The temperature is nearly perfect today too. Cool and slightly breezy, although it warms up a bit when the gentle wind stops.

A quick note on camping spots past Lake Morena. There are many unmarked tent spots for miles north of town. Many are not even marked on Guthooks or the Halfmile maps. If you do not want to stay in Lake Morena and have enough water until the next source, keep trekking and you'll find great places to lay your head.

One thing I love to do while hiking is to take a moment to look back to see how far I've come. It's a little shocking sometimes to see a distant hill or mountain that you know you climbed up and over to get to where you are. It also shows you how much a human body can do by simply putting one foot in front of the other. For the most part, the trail today has been well groomed which makes it easy to keep your miles per hour pace up and make great progress. When it's a rocky or rough trail, not so much.

Water in the desert creates gorgeous green areas – wooded glens, shaded brooks, etc. Literally, this can happen around the shoulder of a hill, one moment you are in dry, hot chaparral, the next you are under trees with the temperature cooling. I'm not sure which road it was, but it crossed a bridge that spanned above our heads as we hiked and stopped at the water source that ran below it. Many hikers stopped to soak their feet in the cool stream. The pylons holding up the bridge were covered in graffiti – some from PCT hikers. The locals allegedly say it's OK for PCT hikers to write on them – a trail register of a sort. However, others in the hiking community say it's not practicing Leave No Trace if you write on them. I did not have a sharpie on me in any case, so I did not sign.

I sat under this bridge in the shade, between a split watercourse on a little, sandy island and ate an early lunch; leftover pizza from the malt shop. It still tasted fabulous. As I was busy stuffing my face and enjoying my time out of the sun, I spied Erick/Dutchman upstream, spreading out his gear to dry in the sunshine. He came over to chat for a bit. Apparently, he had a lot of condensation issues the night before and was taking the opportunity to get his gear dry while taking a break.

Too soon I was done with lunch, packed up and used strategically placed rocks to cross to the other side of the stream, reluctantly leaving the shade. The next water crossing was a small river 2 miles ahead. It wasn't flowing fast but looked deep with lots of underwater snags. Some nice person had dragged a long two-by-four across to the other side of the bank. It was wobbly, but workable. I don't have the best balance but managed to get across without falling in, cheered on by two fellow hikers. They were a couple – and I feel terrible, but I can't remember either of their names. I *think* the woman's name was Jessica (no trail name yet), and her Instagram name was Phantomferns or something similar. My memory aside, they were nice people, and way faster hikers than me.

Next stop was Boulder Oaks, a wonderful, shady campground with horse corrals, clean pit toilets, and a water spigot. This campground is a great stopping point if you don't want to stay at Lake Morena and can knock out another 6 miles. It was far too early in the day to make camp, so a lot of us rested there while filtering water and moved on. The rest of the trail was a climb from Highway 8 toward Mt. Laguna. The trail ascended steeply from the highway for a good mile, then became a bit more gradual, but still a rough climb. Or at least classified as 'butt burner' level.

Later, from high on a ridge above, I could see several hikers frolicking in Kitchen Creek down in the canyon. It looked enticing, but the trail down to it was steep and sketchy. I was exhausted and didn't feel like it was a good idea to try to clamber down to the large creek, blowing out a kneecap and then trudge back up. Plus, I knew I wanted to make the Fred Canyon campsites before the end of the day and time was a-wastin'! If I stopped here, I definitely would not make it before dark. Still, the creek looked tempting. I could see others down there sunbathing. Reports say that Fred Canyon also had a well flowing stream, so maybe I can look forward to soaking my aching feet there in a few miles. I doubt it's big enough to swim in, but I can sure use something to soak my entire body in. The trail has been mainly doing nothing but gaining elevation since Highway 8.

There's a small road ahead that I have to cross and I spied a small igloo off to the side of the trail. I got excited, as this could be my first experience with trail magic! A small trash bag was next to it full of empty Gatorade bottles, weighed down by one corner of the igloo. Imaging a refreshingly cool Gatorade, I opened the igloo and... IT WAS EMPTY! Noooooo! Argh. All it contained was melted water from ice cubes. (Yes, I scooped some of this out for use later because it was still cool.) Disappointed, I crossed the road and continued climbing the trail. Thirty minutes later, a couple of hikers passed me and said that the trail angel driving a jeep had literally just refilled the igloo. Argh again! Impeccable timing on my part.

Nearing Fred Canyon

I made it to Fred Canyon before dark and completed the 12 miles. My body feels all 12 miles and is a bit sore, yet I am proud that I managed to get to my goal for the day. Even sore as I am, I think the day went pretty well. The first 6 miles were pretty 'chill', then the climb began. It was bad, not 'Hauser canyon' bad, but challenging. There are a lot of hikers camping here and more showing up searching for a place to set up their tent or hammock as darkness descends. I tried to prop my feet over a log while lying back onto my pack to ease the swelling and soreness of my feet. I didn't want to move again, but know I have to get my tent set up before I lose daylight. Meh.

A little south of Fred Canyon along the PCT

Fred Canyon is a nice green spot for camping. Speaking of 'green'... There is a heavy marijuana presence on the PCT. It's always been that way from what I've heard, but now that it's recreationally legal in California, as well as Oregon and Washington, it may be more widespread. Not that I mind, after all I voted to legalize it since I was old enough to vote. Now, as a fifty-year-old, it's nice to see it legal and regulated as liquor is. Because there are so many hikers camping at this location tonight, you bet it um...well the campground had a peculiar scent about it for a while.

As I write this, the cacophony of snoring has begun. A guy in a tent next to me sounds like an extra from The Walking Dead as his snores rip into the night sounding like a loud, hissing zombie. Ugh.

It's going to be a long night.

April 11th, 2019

Worst night of sleep. A whopping two hours. It was cold last night, and it seemed like everyone snored around me, not just the 'zombie' snorer. I lounged around longer than I wanted to because of being so tired and only managed to break camp at 8 AM. I should be able to make Mount Laguna today, 10-11 miles ahead, mostly uphill, but I'm worried about my knees. They are a little swollen this morning from the 12 miles I did yesterday. Hopefully the lack of sleep doesn't slow me down too much either.

The morning warmed up quickly after I started out and I had to do a wardrobe change less than a mile from camp. Off came the extra layers, on went the sunglasses and I took a few moments to rub on some sunscreen as the blazing ball of fire rose in the sky.

There is an infamous sign along this stretch warning of a safety hazard in the area for unexploded military ordnance and encourages hikers to not stray from the trail. Several years ago, an Apache helicopter crashed during an exercise and some of the ordinance it carried was scattered over the region. The military was unable to find it all, but the PCT and the dirt roads in the area were declared safe. There is a level dirt area past the sign, along a dirt road for vehicles, although there are no cars here right now. The trail winds its way up a hillside after the sign and keeps climbing through chaparral. After a half mile or so, I pause to look back at my progress this morning. Can you guess what I see? A truck parked below, handing out trail magic sodas and taking hiker's pictures. It seems I've missed trail magic yet again! I know, I know. You can't and shouldn't rely on this 'magic', but I could really use a pick-me-up about now.

My knees are more swollen now, I really need to elevate and ice them – or at least rest and use my small supply of KT tape. There's no opportunity for rest yet though, so I keep pushing. One thing that takes my mind off my aches and pains are the jaw dropping views. My eyes trace the trail ahead as it hugs the rising hills.

The sound of three hikers makes its way up the trail behind me and eventually I 'pull over' to let them pass as they approach. A guy and two women thank me as they pass, the last one had a chipper English accent that was vaguely familiar. I look squarely at her and realize it is Mary Mansfield, another YouTube vlogger, from the UK. I said hi and had a brief chat with her as they were powering up the hill – I never saw her again after but that is not surprising. She's a fast hiker and all three of them were up and over this portion of the trail while I sat on a rock for lunch watching. She is just as sweet and nice as she comes across on her vlogs.

I have to say here again, if I haven't already, that most hikers pass me as I'm not a very fast hiker. I'm determined and can put a lot of hours in, but my pace is not very fast. Especially going up steep pulls. Despite being slow, I'm surprised when I overtake Mando, otherwise known as "Cuban Fiber" (I think he prefers Mando). He had found a strong cell signal and was live on a social media platform. I think, but am not sure, that he was the fellow snoring like a zombie nearby at the Fred Canyon campsite. I greeted him as I passed and later took a break along the trail, only to have him pass me later. This is called "leapfrogging" and happens a lot when you are near hikers that hike around your own pace. He's young though, and I don't anticipate being able to stay caught up with him for long.

Ending my break, a section hiker stopped when I was pulling on the pack to continue and talked about the trail. And talked. And talked… and talked. He moved on eventually and found Mando on a switchback above me and proceeded to talk, and talk, and talk. Don't get me wrong, I'm all for socializing while hiking. It helps the time go faster. However, there's a tipping point where you need to be alone. At least for me, being the introvert that I am.

Ahead, I hear Mando saying, "I'm just here for some solitude. Can't I get some solitude?"

The other man agreed with the sentiment before continuing to talk at him. I say *at* him because it was pretty much a one-way conversation.

I round the corner of the trail and see Mando on his phone and the other hiker moving on. This struck me as strange because I was pretty sure we had lost that cell signal we had earlier.

"Hey Mando – we have signal here too?" I asked.

In a low voice, "No maaan. I couldn't get him to leave me alone, so I faked a call."

I laughed so much and kept chuckling for a while after that. I ended up leapfrogging the section hiker and learned a lot about this section of the trail, but it still took him a long time to move on. Mando passed me too. I have no idea if he met up with the section hiker again or not.

It's still early in the day and I'm starting to tire out already, around mile 36. Dang – not sure if I can make Mount Laguna today. It's too soon to stop yet though. I have to keep pushing.

Close to mile 38 there is a water source and a climb afterward. As I approached the area, I heard a distant cheer from Mando high above me along the trail, telling me I can make it. I smiled and waved at him before trudging on to the stream to filter water. I removed my shoes and socks and rested my feet as I drank water and snacks. So far, I have been lucky and dodged any blisters. However, I have unfortunately developed ingrown nails on a few toes, which are becoming infected. Not sure how to fix this problem as it's near impossible to keep feet clean while thru-hiking. It seems like we take dirt baths given the amount of dirt we have on us at any given time.

Finishing filtering water, I get ready to head up from the stream and who do I see coming up behind me but Erick! I hadn't seen him since leaving the water source under the bridge early yesterday. He camped a few miles before Fred

Canyon. I must be moving really slow today. I know he is fast on ascents, but I should have had a 3-mile head start according to him. Oh well, it's not a competition, but I sure do wish I wasn't so slow at times. He stops to begin filtering water while I begin to struggle up the trail again.

I found a good-sized washout of the trail caused by the heavy winter rain the region received this year. It wasn't too bad as I was able to jump across easily with a heavy pack.

Later, Erick 'leapfrogged' me and was planning to camp a couple miles before town if he didn't make it into Mount Laguna that day. I told him I'd try to camp at the same point too but wasn't sure I could even make it that far. I was fading fast. I'm beyond frustrated as it's only around 4 PM, but the lack of sleep is hitting me hard. The next marked camp on the map is close to mile 39, but at this point, I'm on the lookout for any unmarked, remote site that I could call home for the night. Preferably, a site with some wind blocking features.

There is a comment on the Guthooks map app about a large, flat area ideal for camping that isn't on the map at about mile 38.8. I found it just off to the left of the PCT with several potential spots to pitch a tent. All flat. All surrounded by manzanitas, a couple larger trees and scrub brush to block wind. An added bonus was a mountain meadow beyond the trees. Just beautiful. I picked a tent site near a healthy tree and tall surrounding bushes to serve as a wind block. Tomorrow will be a short day for me – 3 to 4 miles to reach Mount Laguna. Nero day coming!

I set up my tent and got to work on dinner. This will be my first night making mac and cheese, which I bought from Costco. There's a funny story behind this. I saw a bucket... a 27 lb. bucket of mac and cheese for sale there and thought it would be the perfect hiking food for the PCT. Not every day, but near enough. I've been teased about buying it, but absolutely love it. Tonight was the first time I cooked it while on trail. It ended up being a little al dente, but I ate it all anyway.

Yum! Delicious, but a bit of a messy clean up.

Falling another day behind on the hike worries me. In my head I keep thinking I should be in Mount Laguna by now, or beyond. I'm not sure I can make it to Canada at this rate with small mileage days like this. Oh well, I hope to make it as far as I can, given the time that I have to hike the PCT.

***

In order to attempt this thru hike, I made arrangements at work by taking all my saved vacation days and then an unpaid leave of absence until the third week of September. I could not ask for more and still have my job guaranteed when I returned. Honestly, at the time and on paper, this seems like plenty of time to complete a thru hike. Two days behind though from week one is getting me nervous, as I don't know if I'll ever pick up enough speed to make the lost time up or avoid more delays in the future.

All I can do is try and try, I shall.

Chapter Three
Mount Laguna

April 12th 2019

    Today should be a nice and short day into Mount Laguna, about 4 miles. No one camped with me at this wonderful campsite last night. Bummer, it's an excellent spot! I slept like a wee baby – just blissful sleep which helped make up for the night before. I can't stress enough what a great semi secluded site this was. There is plenty of room for many tents. I slept in a little too much though and did not get out of camp until 8:20 AM. Oopsie.
    Checking my finger and toenails I found I'm getting nail infections in both. Every night I try to wipe them down with wet wipes, but I think I'm prone to ingrown nails and you simply can't keep clean enough out here. Hikers are dirt magnets no matter how meticulous you are about hygiene. I need a long shower to help clean the nails.
    Fresh legs this morning make all the difference in the world with uphill hiking. The incline isn't bothering me much at all.
    Glancing back from where I started today after covering some territory, I see beautiful clouds cresting the top of the not-so-distant coastal range of mountains to the

west. These views are one main reason that I'm out here. Just breathtaking.

As I go up in elevation, I notice the surroundings change from mostly chaparral brush to pine trees. It is still dry, but this is what you would typically see in southern California mountain towns. With the gain in altitude, the temperature cools and makes the hike delightful.

Forested trail nearing Mount Laguna

The cooler weather, a good night's sleep and a soft trail full of pine needle duff also makes for a quick hike. I clocked myself at more than 2 miles an hour. Going uphill! See, I *can* make good time… if everything aligns perfectly. Ha! It's not like that usually, I know.

I ran into a couple of hikers headed south – unsure if they were day hikers or section south bounders. One of them had seen my YouTube channel and recognized me. I'm a little surprised at this since I have only a few hundred subscribers right now. He encouraged me to keep pushing on and the short meeting gave me a little more pep in my step as

I got closer to Mt Laguna. Later, I met another hiker named "Medicine Man" near where the trail split to head toward the campground and town. He is hiking in sandals! I bet his feet are nice and cool right now, if a little dirty.

The edge of the Burnt Rancheria Campground came into sight, the trail heading almost directly to a restroom. A large sigh of relief escaped my lips as I made a beeline to the toilets, practically running. One effect of hiking a long trail is a natural 'triggering' of those urges when you see a viable pit toilet, or even better, a real one with running water. I can't tell you how happy I am when I run across one while hiking.

Ahhh, the things you take for granted...

Washing up, I then continued to walk into the town proper with Medicine Man and passed by the Pine Tavern Café, which was closed. There was a sign that said they should be open by noon. Since I had time to kill, I decided to make the road walk further into town to find the general store to resupply for the next leg of the journey. It seemed like a looooong walk along an asphalt road. The store appeared, large by small town standards, and seems to carry anything a hiker would need. Many people were lounging on the front porch and organizing food in their packs. I went inside, signed the trail register and shuffled my tired legs around, picking out favorites to feed me until Julian and some extra food for today to snack on while waiting on the Pine Tavern to open. The store is 'pricey' but has a great selection. There is a post office in town, but the cost of sending a priority mail parcel compared to the store prices makes the cost essentially the same. So, I decided to support the locals and not mail a resupply box to this location.

One corner of the store also holds a neat collection of antiques. (Not for sale as far as I know.)

After making my purchases, I sat on the porch among the other hikers and sorted through my new haul of food and combined bags to consolidate items and save weight. For example, I took three bags of chips I had bought and dumped them all into a gallon Ziploc bag, tossing the original containers. Mixed salty goodness.

I met so many other hikers today in town, even Seraina who I shared the tent with at Scout and Frodo's. Yes, she had caught up to me (not surprising as she's a young, strong hiker and I am not). There also was another young man who used an older, external frame backpack. You know, the type of pack you may remember from the 1970s. Heavy and sturdy. He had a trail name already, "Old School" of course.

Sadly, I do not have a 'trail family' yet, but I can see some of these people becoming part of one with me... if only I could keep up!

Let me pause and explain to those who do not know what a 'trail family' is, also referred to as a 'Tramily'. It is hard to put into words but think of a small or large group of strangers who meet while hiking (although you could hit the trail with a significant other or friend too), who decide to start camping and hiking the trail together. Normally, they all are capable of hiking the same number of miles per day and keep similar paces. You may or may not actually be hiking side by side with them, but you run in to each other at break spots and always try to camp together. There also is a fantastic bond that forms between the members of the trail family and many remain close friends after hiking together for so long.

Still consolidating my food, I saw Erick coming back from the post office while sitting on the porch of the store. I'm not sure if he's moving on this afternoon since we got to town so early or if he was going to take a 'nero' day and stay at the lodge or campground. A 'nero' is when you take most of the day off after getting into town – or sometimes getting a very late start after a town stay. Not quite a 'zero' day of hiking no trail miles, but near enough. He said he was planning on staying at the lodge if there were any rooms still available, but was unsure and he may push on.

Around the time it was scheduled to open, I trudged back up the road to the Pine Tavern Café and met a group of new hikers waiting in front. Opening time came and went and we still waited. Eventually an employee came out and said that a cook had called out sick and that it will be a delayed opening. Ugh, we were all starving, but didn't want a sick cook making food for us either. Resolved to wait, we lounged on the grass at the corner of the property for a long time talking and napping...until it started to rain. By then, many other hikers had joined us, stomachs growling. Thankfully, the restaurant has a covered porch area for outdoor eating, so we fled the rain and huddled together under cover. Three hours later...yes *three* hours later, the restaurant opened their doors and started taking orders. They knew they had a large group of hungry hikers on their hands and instead of table orders, wrote down what we wanted as we walked in, then handed the ticket to the kitchen to prepare. We didn't pay until they called us up to the bar area after they served the food. It was a weird set up, but probably the fastest way of getting grub out to us. Their system worked well in hindsight. I don't think they take orders this way normally, but only when slammed with many hungry mouths to feed. I crammed down a great tasting burger and order of fries.

Last night, I had a limited signal at the camping spot I was at and I used it to look around Mount Laguna for places to stay if I decided to have a roof over my head rather than a tent spot in the campground. The lodge I mentioned before had a tendency to sell out. Mount Laguna is very small, but I decided to try looking at my Airbnb app and see if I had as much luck with it as I had in Lake Morena. I was surprised to see a few listings right behind the Pine Tavern Café. There is an old RV park at the rear of it that the current owner is slowly converting into a Tiny Home community and at least two were ready and available to rent for tonight. Compared to the house in Lake Morena, the Tiny Home was expensive – more than twice the amount. It turned out to be a freezing cold night, so I don't know if I would have been better off staying in the campground or not in that temperature. Yet the house had problems, not the least of which was a water main break that left me with no water for several hours. Thankfully, I had taken a quick shower and finished doing 'sink' laundry before the water stopped. There was advertised laundry, but no change machines in the small room when I found it – so 'sink laundry' it had to be. The color of the water after washing was nearly black. It's amazing how much filth and dirt you attract after a few days of hiking.

Overall, it just was not a good stay. The small space heater kept the place warm enough but took a few hours to get the place comfortable. Still, it was better than shivering in my tent all night.

It was bitter cold tonight, too. I returned to the Pine Tavern Café for dinner and hot chocolate wearing my sleeping layer while they were attempting to fix the water break at the tiny home. I'm sure I looked a bit silly with my loud print fleece bottoms and bright red merino wool long sleeve shirt with a silver puffy jacket on top. Even so, I felt like I fit right in with all the other hikers tonight wearing similar cold weather attire before heading back to the rental.

The tiny home is close enough to the tavern to get the Wi-Fi I purchased earlier that day for twelve hours, but the signal must be throttled because I could not get anything uploaded to YouTube no matter how many hours I tried. That purchase was a waste of money. My phone is running out of storage space for my photos and videos and I need to get data up and out in order to make room for more.

Settling down now on a comfy mattress next to a space heater back in the tiny home… I can't sit up in bed, it's too tight a space with less head room than my tent, yet I think I'm going to sleep very well tonight.

April 13th, 2019

I went back through the campground this morning to reach the branch in the trail and pick up where I left off on the PCT. Don't miss this portion of the trail and skip ahead to the end of town, it has some amazing views.

After moving past Mount Laguna, the trail becomes wooded and very pretty. On and off the occasional hiker would pass me as I sauntered along, enjoying the soft duft underfoot. I enjoyed hiking through dappled shade – a rarity on the desert portion of the PCT. Too soon, it switched back to chaparral and sun. However, today seems like the perfect temperature day for hiking... so far not hot and not cold. I'll take it!

I came around a corner of a large hill and suddenly saw San Jacinto waaaaaaay in the distance.

Home! Baby, I'm coming! It may take me awhile yet, but I'm coming.

This was the first view of San Jacinto since leaving home in the Coachella Valley for Scout and Frodo's house. I'm a little shocked that it's already visible. Have I made that much progress already? Not that it's close, but the fact that I can see it...

That wasn't the end of the drop-dead gorgeous vistas. After reaching a ridgeline the view was astounding. Several hikers sat taking breaks gazing at the view of Mt. San Jacinto, Mt. San Gorgonio, the Santa Rosa range, the Salton Sea and the desert spread out far below. The scenery was windy and breathtaking. It was uplifting to sit and contemplate the majestic panorama of mountains and desert valleys below. I didn't know most of the hikers hanging out here, but saw a lone tent being packed up by none other than Mando. He skipped staying in town and slept here on this windy ridgeline. But, oh, what a view he must have woken up to in the morning.

If it wasn't so early in the day, I may have stayed and enjoyed the view for a while, content to fill my heart with the amazing landscape. Yet the need to make miles pushed me onward. Leaving, I headed downhill until 'nature called' and I dropped my pack and pulled out my P-Style. This device is one of the best inventions ever made for women who camp and hike. At the risk of too much information, I will say that... oh well this entire section may be TMI, so I'll just lay it out like it is. The P-Style is a long, 'half pipe' shaped piece of plastic that enables women to urinate while standing up. Unlike funnels, it doesn't get overwhelmed by what you put into it. However, if you don't position it correctly, you may have similar problems. During this particular trip behind tall brush, I had those problems. Its unusual when this happens, but... well let's just say I ended up with lots of pee down my britches and legs.

Delightful. (*Sarcasm.*)

I froze trying to figure out what to do. Hike on and hope no one catches up while my pants were wet or hide behind the bushes for a lengthy period of time waiting for them to dry? Should I tie them up to fly in the wind from a bush – a semi wet flag warning all that hike by not to interact with the mortified hiker lurking behind a screen of creosote?

A tree stump stood near the trail where my 'accident' occurred, and I decided it was time for an early lunch ten feet off the trail where other hikers may not see my pants as I waited for them to dry a little. The sun was out. My hope was that things would dry out quickly. Thankfully, my pants were better (not perfect), by the time I finished lunch and I set out again, not as worried that someone would hike up behind me and see wet britches. I further distracted myself from embarrassment by looking down at the desert floor far below the trail, bursting with yellow flowers. The views along this trail can be stunning and used as a tool to distract yourself from achy muscles or extreme embarrassment.

Setting out again, I knew I was getting close to the 50-mile marker. In the grand scheme of things, it's not a lot of miles, but felt like a large milestone to me. As I approached it, I saw a tent far off to the left of the pathway. A hiker had either called it a day already or was getting a very late start. He came over to chat as I turned a corner on the trail, and I saw "50" outlined in stones. It still snuck up on me even though I knew it was getting close. Another hiker who I met back in Mount Laguna at the Café came up behind and offered to take a photo with my phone of me next to the mile marker. He claimed to be a slow hiker, but of course he was still light-years faster than me. At least I kept him in sight for quite some time after our photo ops.

Author at the 50 mile 'marker'

Horses! Yes, horses! I think I mentioned it before, but the PCT is also an equestrian trail. Most of the path is shared with them and you will run across horses, or at least signs of them on the ground along the way. I saw a cluster of four before I hit mile 52, a sign announcing that there was now only a mere 2600 miles until we reached Canada. Further along, there was a short spur trail to the Pioneer Mail Picnic area. Many of us decided to hang out and relax there under shade trees, eat and socialize. There was also a water spigot which set us up nicely with water until the next source. I didn't know any of these hikers, most where new faces. This group made me feel old too. Most were 20-somethings...none close to my age.

More great views of the desert opened up after leaving the picnic area while climbing an abandoned cliff road. Near the top of the climb, memorials stood along the side of the road marking deaths of loved ones both human and non-human. Well, it is a beautiful place for them – overlooking a fabulous desert vista.

The trail runs along some cool cliffsides a bit beyond the memorials after climbing up and around a hill. Call me weird, but I love a good cliffside trail with a sheer drop to one side. As long as it is maintained of course and not washed out!

Toward the end of the day, I noticed soreness in both calves and infections throbbing on the ingrown toenails with a vengeance. Ugh. Here we go again.

Today, I'm trying to make the Oriflamme campsite. The site is a bit exposed and set around boulders, but I've heard that if you have a view of Oriflamme Mountain at night that you can see the 'Ghost Lights' it is famous for. The name actually means "Golden Flame". There are lots of stories regarding what causes the sparks or lights to appear, the scientific explanation is that they are static electricity that sometimes can be seen when the desert sands blow against the quartz in the mountain. I'm not sure how often the phenomenon happens, but it doesn't look like I'm going to make it to that campground anyway. I want to make it to Julian tomorrow, but I can't see myself doing a 20+ mile day just yet.

The shadows are getting long and I'm trying to find a decent place to set up camp. I passed a dry riverbed that had a few tents along it. There didn't seem to be more room, although I'm sure I could have squeezed my one-person tent there somewhere if I was desperate. I wasn't yet and plodded on.

Thankfully, not too much further, I found a small space literally alongside the trail that was mostly flat and large enough for my small tent. I'm not sure exactly how far I was from the Oriflamme camp sites, but I was beat, and this looked like a good site even though I'd be by myself.

I wanted to make it further today. Even so, this ended up being my biggest day yet – 14 miles! Getting stronger every day.

There are not many private areas at this site to take care of the call of nature, but I'll manage. At least I can see for a long distance in either direction before attempting anything under the cover of darkness tonight. I had to test this at least once overnight when I stumbled out of the tent to pee in the dark and later do more. I was really worried about a night hiker coming by, so kept an eye peeled for the light of a headlamp cresting the brush.

Lots of night noises tonight, coyote yipping and once, a distinct howl of a pack of something more. They didn't sound like coyotes, but perhaps wolves in the mountains far away. Are there wolves out here? I don't even know.

Surprisingly, I fell asleep easily. Throughout the night I found that the site was not as flat as I originally believed it to be. I woke up frequently with my face plastered against tent wall from slipping ever so slowly on the slightly slanted ground. The solitude of the site lulled me quickly back into the ether after adjusting my position.

April 14th, 2019

I had a good night's sleep last night. There was cell signal, so I was also able to upload video to YouTube and make more room on my phone's storage for more clips. Footsteps went by my tent before dawn and caused me to start moving. My goal was always to be hiking on the trail before the sun reared its head over the horizon, but it hadn't happened yet.

After eating a little breakfast, I started breaking camp. A hiker appeared over the hill south of me on trail and walked by as I was stuffing my belongings into my pack. She stopped for a second to say hi and then continued walking. I recognized her from Mount Laguna outside of the Pine Tavern Café where all the hikers waited in the rain for the restaurant to open. We will keep 'leapfrogging' each other on the trail today. Her trail name was unofficially 'Easy Peasy', but I think she preferred to go by her civilian name of 'Chantel'. She hikes a bit faster than me, but close enough to my pace that I have hopes of getting to know someone and hiking with them on and off.

The trail is beautiful this morning, winding through boulder fields, and running along long ridges. You can see the path cut into the mountain sides for miles and miles ahead. Yuccas were in bloom, bursting with white and sometimes pink blossoms.

Yellow flowers near mile marker 60

Let's talk about hiking uphill. One thing that you cannot prepare for if you only do day hikes before heading to the PCT is the never-ending elevation gains. Sure, you go downhill too, but inevitably you will always have an uphill section following. It is just the way the trail is, you go up and down constantly and rarely have a long flat section. Mentally, I hope I'm at the end of a long climb, but there is always another even if you do 'finish' one. Unless the grade is very gentle, I feel every step of those climbs.

Today promises to be very water centric. It's warm, but not brutally hot and there are not many natural water sources along the trail until you reach the highway where you can hitch into Julian or the Stagecoach RV park. At mile 59ish there's a spur trail that takes you to the Sunrise Trailhead that has a tank with a water spigot hidden under the lip. Earlier that morning, I had told Chantel that I likely would skip that source but decided otherwise as I approached where the trail split off. I was ahead of Chantel and could see her with another hiker behind me on the trail a half mile or so. I danced and waved, pointing towards the spur trail, trying to communicate that I was indeed going there. I'm not sure if she understood me, but she did not appear at the tank later. I sat there, taking a long break along with others, having lunch. The water source is a gross horse trough that hikers use for water. The spigot under the lip puts out fresher water, but it is still wise to filter.

I met a couple of German men hiking together at the trailhead that I'd seen before back in Mt. Laguna. I'm horrible with names, unless they have trail names, which they didn't have yet at that point. Both were friendly and always said "Hi" when they passed me or when I caught up to them (usually at water sources). They left soon after I arrived to get back on the trail and make progress. Because this stretch promised to be dry, I started carrying 4.5 liters of water to make sure I made it to the next reliable source. That's a heavy water haul – over 8 lbs. of water. Oh well. Totally worth it in my mind knowing my water intake.

Shale and loose rocks sat along this stretch of trail on and off, alternating with a decently groomed pathway. My ankles are not happy with me – this is definitely making it a more challenging hike than the norm. When you have to think about where and how you're placing your feet, it takes much more energy than when you're walking in 'cruise control'.

Oh, and speaking of unhappy ankles – add unhappy knees and feet to my list of ailments after one particular downhill that was steep and beat the heck out of them, even while using trekking poles to lessen the impact. At the bottom of this there was a hot and dry stream bed where several people rested in small patches of shade. Chantel was there! (She did not go to the Sunrise highway stop.) Erick was there too! I hadn't seen him since Mount Laguna. They both said there was a slow trickle of water fifty yards up the dry creek bed. I trudged up, collected water to filter and sat down to rest and eat. The two German hikers were there as well and again left as soon as I arrived, so I began teasing them that they always seem to leave when I caught up to them and was beginning to take it personally. They chuckled and went on their way.

The next 3 miles consisted of a constant climb up the trail, the beginning of which was painfully steep. Taken first thing in the morning would be one story, but in the afternoon with tired legs, not so much. I continue to struggle going uphill... in fact at this time of day it's pure torture. Erick and Chantel started the climb with me. He soon left us in the dust as he does well on uphills at *any* time of day. He seems to fly up them! Chantel and I struggled together, the sun pounding on our heads. In fact, I don't know what I would have done at that point without her as a hiking partner. I know I was muttering out loud at the misery I was going through and even though she was not happy about the situation either, helped keep me going with positive affirmations until we found a decent camp spot.

My knees are beat up today – I blame having to shuffle downhill before the wash. Generally, hiking downhill doesn't bother my legs much, but this one was brutal. I'm contemplating doing a "Zero" day in Julian even though I hadn't planned on doing one this early in the hike. A zero day is when you rest and do absolutely no trail miles, although you generally are walking around doing errands (laundry, food, etc.). I'll reach the road that leads to Julian tomorrow.

Before mile marker 66, there was a flat area where the trail turns, hugging two hills with enough flat spots for five or six tents. The two German gentlemen were there already set up for the evening. It didn't take any convincing for me and Chantel to stop for the day. Erick had kept going, powering up the next climb. This was a dry camp, meaning no water nearby, but you get used to that on the PCT and plan accordingly when you come across water sources. It was still light after Chantel and I set up our tents, but she called it a night to get some early rest as she planned on getting a pre-dawn start. I shuffled around for a bit after eating dinner and edited a video in the tent before trying to sleep. No other hikers camped at that spot, just me, Chantel and the two German men.

When I realized that I had signal (surprisingly in this sheltered area), I uploaded a video to YouTube and contemplated calling ahead to Julian to reserve a room as the town is notorious for accommodations being sold out. I had a list of places to stay with me from a guidebook many people use on the trail (Yogi's) and called the first hotel on the list, the historic Julian Gold Rush Hotel. I tried them first not just because of its history and that they fed you breakfast and snacks for teatime, but the fact that there was laundry service there. No one else in town had that, so I thought it was worth a try. I was extremely lucky as they had a room available for not only one, but two nights. Did I really want to zero this early? Looking down at my swollen knees, I bit the financial bullet and asked for the second night as well. It's not terribly expensive, but not cheap either. In the end, I knew I physically needed a break and planned to not spend as much later down the line during the hike.

Even though the second half of my day was miserable, I was thankful to settle down to sleep in my snug tent and toasty quilt.

Chapter Four
Julian

April 15th, 2019

Today will be the final push into Julian. I saw Chantel quietly take off from camp as I opened my tent to cook a little breakfast in the early hours. She waved and began the climb in the cool morning. I managed to pack everything up and get started by 7:15 AM, probably the earliest time yet. I even beat one of the German's out of camp for a little bit of a head start.

Oh, don't worry, he will pass me within the first hour or so, I'm sure.

My toes are weird. You'd think all this hiking would give me blisters. I don't have any yet, but ouch – those ingrown and infected nails hurt. It's next to impossible to keep everything clean. I'm looking forward to the hotel stay to dry out the feet and get them squeaky clean for a day. I'm also looking forward to Julian for fresh food, especially their famous pies!

It's a cool morning... so far... for the initial climb out of camp. I have convertible hiking pants that can be changed into shorts when the weather warms up, but I couldn't find one of the 'legs' this morning, so am braving the nippy morning in shorts. Better chilly than hot, I guess. Or I could have started a new fashion trend on the trail wearing one full leg and the other bare. Hmmm.

Oh hey, I must let you all know to not always believe the people who say the trail is *all* downhill from Mount Laguna to Julian. Uh... NOT. It's not as bad as the pull up into Mount Laguna, but it's definitely *not* all downhill.

So far, it's a nice day, not too hot and so clear you can see the trail for miles as it hugs the hillsides.

The Rodriguez Road marker appears as I approach the next water cache. It's pretty famous on vlogs – basically looks like a home-made street sign in the middle of the desert marking the intersection of dirt roads. There's a cluster of other hikers finishing filtering their water at the cache, my supply isn't too bad, but I plan to top it off and keep going. There's not enough shade to comfortably rest here. This is the last water until Scissors Crossing, past mile 77. This is not always a reliable cache, but I can see it is doing well today with several full gallons as I walked up and dropped my pack. The cache is made up of semi empty gallon jugs that are set up one by one to catch a slow drip from a black pipe sticking out of a cement block. A note from a trail angel asks the hikers to replace any full gallon jug with an empty one to keep the water filling up various bottles instead of overflowing and going to waste. I hunker down and filter water after swapping out one of the bottles.

Continuing on the trail I reach the coolest part of the hike so far today. I mean 'cool' as in 'awesome', not temperature of course (the cool morning had dissipated long ago). This was my first sketchy ridgeline walk! It was narrow with crumbling trail at some points and steep drop offs – pretty neat (sorry mom). I had to use one trekking pole on the upslope side to anchor me while balancing with the other on the downslope side. This was a favorite portion of the trail for me today. There was another woman that I briefly hiked with in this section named Catherine who did not like the heights and was *not* a happy hiker during these miles.

Flat 'pancake' cacti grew all over the hills and beside the trail with deep pink buds growing along its edges making them look a little like hands (they are called a Prickly Pear Cactus). I must be craving fruit because they look like little raspberries right now. Am I that hungry?

My mind starts to drift as I impatiently wait for the long flat I know is coming a few miles before Scissors Crossing and then town soon after that. It's amazing how far you can hike in a day, or so it seems. In reality, a person can spend miles and miles winding your way up and down on the PCT. No one said the trail was a straight line – and it's a good thing it isn't otherwise it would be overly steep.

PCT northbound toward Julian...

Four or five miles to go now until Scissors Crossing – it seems like an endless day. The heat has returned too, but at least there's a slight breeze to help cool things down. Eventually I reach the bottom of the valley and winced while starting the long flat march to the road a couple miles distant. My feet hurt, my knees ache – heck everything is killing me at this point. I was alone for quite some time on this part of the trail until I heard somebody approaching me from behind. My pace must have really fallen off since this morning. I pause and step to the side of the trail to let the hiker pass and look up to see Mando.

Hey Mando!

He is sweating like a beast, but on a mission to make town and is moving fast. I soon lose sight of him and by the time I reach Scissors Crossing he has already gotten a hitch into town.

Before I climbed up to the road to try to hitch too (first time I've *ever* hitchhiked in my life), I waved at a few hikers under the bridge of the highway where a large water cache resided. I talked to a hiker named Chris who was looking for Chantel. She had also hiked with her a couple days before. I told her that we'd camped together but she was far ahead of me today. The fact that Chris hadn't seen her meant that she more than likely hitched at an earlier road crossing into the Stagecoach RV park to stay there instead of coming to the highway to try to get into Julian. Chris also said she recognized me from my vlog channel. Again, I was surprised! I don't think I'll ever get used to that.

Chris said she was going to hang out under the bridge for a bit longer before heading into town. I was tempted to stay, socialize, and rest there in the shade also, but really, *really* wanted to get into town, check in to my hotel and get some real food. A shower would follow, but not right away. We all smelled at this point, so it really did not matter much. I'm starting to learn that food was always *the* priority when in town.

Both of us exchanged cell numbers so we could let each other know if we saw or heard from Chantel. Each of us gave Chantel our numbers a couple days ago, so one of us was bound to hear from her after sending text messages. (Much later that day we found out she was indeed staying at Stagecoach and would not be going to Julian.)

Now, time to hitchhike!

I have never hitch hiked before and was nervous as I was doing it solo. As a precaution, I slipped my small neck knife I used for slicing cheese and sausage into my pocket. Was I sweating because I was nervous or was it the heat? This goes against everything my parents taught me, "Never take rides from strangers..." etc. In hindsight I had no reason to worry. A car pulled over almost immediately when I put my thumb out. My driver was a sweet older lady named Deb. She dropped me off at my hotel after a nice ride into Julian. The Julian 'Gold Rush' hotel is a historic property built in the late 1800s and is the oldest operating hotel in southern California. It reminds me of an old Victorian home well cared for through the years and modified to house guests. I checked in, dropped my pack, and cleaned up a little. Well... I'll say I *tried* to clean up. I was too hungry to take a shower before heading to Mom's Pie shop for grub, but spent a long time washing my hands and face with real soap. Running water is wonderful, I don't think I'll ever take it for granted now.

Real soap is a luxury most thru-hikers do not use. It's bad for the environment and pollutes water sources. Imagine drinking soap water. Not cool. You get the idea. Plus, water is so scarce in the desert portion of the PCT, you don't want to waste it. Many hikers will use some version of wet wipes, to keep clean.

Mom's Pie is owned by someone who hiked sections of the PCT in the past and hands out a free piece of pie and ice cream along with a drink to hikers if you show your permit. The pies are amazing there! I was starving as well, so I made sure to order a late lunch before getting my free slice of apple pie with cinnamon ice cream and cup of apple cider. While I was getting my food, who came in the door but Erick! He was staying at a different hotel but was there to collect on his free piece of pie also. We sat down together and dug in. The pie and ice cream was heavenly. There's another store in town that gives out a cup of free cider and a small bag of snacks to each PCT hiker that comes in. I was a little late this afternoon to collect that before they closed, but plan on going by tomorrow.

After satisfying my hunger, I wandered next door to a grocer to resupply and later another grocery store further down the street. Next on the 'to-do' list; a delectable shower. The things you take for granted in everyday life end up being pure indulgence while hiking a long trail. My feet look better after the shower, but my toes are still an angry infected red.

Evening fell and I found myself hungry again, so I went out to find dinner to bring back to my room unless I found other hikers that I knew. I ended up at an Italian restaurant and bought an overabundance of food. There were a few hiker looking people there, but no one I knew, so I went back to the room to tackle my salad and pasta alone. I wish I could have coordinated dinner with someone in hindsight (ie. Chris or Erick). But literally, all I could think about after eating today was lying down in bed and resting. I even knocked out for an hour in the late afternoon. There's no TV in the Julian hotel, but that was OK. Besides resting, I recorded a Q&A video for my Vlog and called it a night. Tomorrow, I'm hoping to do a little exploring around Julian on my zero day.

To sum up today, it was full of many highs and lows... the 'lows' were bad, and I considered calling an end to my hike. Not sure why – it wasn't my first bad day, and probably wouldn't be my last, but something is beginning to tip me over the edge. Yes, I'm missing home and Tami, but not to the degree that would drive me off trail. Besides, she did say I had better finish this venture! This was, however, my second day in a row where the last half of the day was miserable.

I must get my head in the right frame of mind. Perhaps the earlier-than-planned zero day here in Julian will help.

April 16th, 2019

Popping my head out to grab an early breakfast, I was surprised by the weather when I opened the hotel room door. Rain, mist, fog and wind. I closed the door and swapped what I was wearing – don't want to ruin my puffy jacket! The Julian hotel has a free breakfast and I took full advantage of that. I think every hiker appreciates a free meal, although this one came with the cost of the hotel room.

The plan today was to rest a lot, but also explore town. Julian had other ideas and the weather continued to be terrible all day long. Basically, I rested in my room for a large part of the day and ventured out when the rain lessened. The cider shop was open, and I guzzled down my free cider and collected a small snack pack of chocolate covered banana chips. It is such a cool little place, I had to buy a few resupply items too. There was an impulse purchase of a 1 lb. bag of black licorice. (Most of that bag ended up in the hotel's hiker box the next morning. I couldn't justify the weight to pack it out no matter how much I like black licorice.)

The theme of today is food. I returned to the hotel and attended the "High Tea" in the afternoon with other hotel guests. The hotel puts out finger food and small sandwiches along with coffee and tea in the late afternoon. Again, it's a free meal for guests. There were a couple other hikers that were partaking of the food and drink, but mostly vacationers. An elderly couple from San Diego County befriended me and talked about their kids and were very interested in hearing me talk about the trail. Near the end of tea, they offered to drive me back to the trailhead tomorrow morning. I was surprised, but secretly crossing my fingers, hoping they were serious about the offer. It would save me hitchhiking back to the trail at Scissors Crossing.

Lounging in bed again after tea, I thought I should take advantage of the fact I was in town and grab some dinner. After all, it's going to be a few days of only trail food starting tomorrow. I ventured out, trying to keep under cover of the store fronts and out of the rain dumping from the sky, while walking down the street looking for a good restaurant. I ducked inside the Julian Café and Bakery, ordered and proceeded to destroy dinner.

I ate so much today; I feel like a stuffed turkey. One thing is for sure, I will sleep well tonight. Well fed, dry and warm.

April 17th, 2019

The hotel had an amazing breakfast this morning. The couple from yesterday were there and followed through on their promise! I feel like I successfully "Yogi'd" a ride from them. Yogi-ing is a term used by thru-hikers to describe convincing other campers/day hikers/anyone to part with a little extra food, drink or just help in general. Think of Yogi the bear trying to get that picnic basket and you have the right idea. Tom and Sue, from the San Diego area, were willing to help and wouldn't take a dime from me when offered as they dropped me off at Scissors Crossing. They were still fascinated by the trail and asked a ton of questions during the drive to learn more, which I tried to answer. When they left Scissors Crossing, they took another female thru hiker back to Julian with them who had hiked in that morning and wanted to get into town. Super kind people.

I am hoping for at least 10 miles today, but also had a late start, hitting the trail at 9:30 AM, so we will see.

The climb out of Scissors Crossing is long, warm and completely exposed to the sun. At least bright splashes of wildflowers help to distract me as I hike up, coloring the hillsides with yellow, white and purple. Ocotillos are blooming red at the end of their tips, and bright purple flowers are bursting from the edges of prickly pear cacti. There are also many caterpillars inching around that will later transform into gypsy moths. Spring in the desert, although hot, can be beautiful.

A Cactus in bloom past Scissors Crossing

I am definitely gaining all the elevation back I lost coming down into Scissors. Whew! For most of the climb you can see a road down below to the left which leads to Warner Springs, the next major stop along the trail. For those of us on the PCT, that will take 2 to 3 days to hike. I look down at the road longingly – a faster, more direct route, but not as pretty. However, I'd be lying if I didn't say I'd rather be on it or even hitch hiking a ride (also called 'yellow blazing') to Warner Springs. This climb is not fun even if I am making decent progress.

Yellow blazing is a term used to describe hikers that skip around parts of the trail by hitchhiking. It is looked down upon by purists who believe if you are thru hiking you should be hiking every inch of open trail. There are always closures that you have to find your way around, but if the trail is open, you should hike it. I'm a bit of a purist, I will admit it. Yet the temptation on a hot day to shorten the distance is real. I can feel all that 'purity' melting under the beating hot sun.

As usual many hikers caught up and passed me. I don't mind too much as I have finally accepted I'm just not as fast as most of the others out here. Three that caught me ended up taking some breaks with me on and off today. Chantel, Chris, and a new lady named Betsy! I thought that Chantel and Chris left yesterday, but they also decided to take a zero day (Chris in Julian and Chantel at the RV park). The new lady was around my age. Betsy, also hiked with the rest of us for the rest of the day. Our paces differed, but often we would sit in small pools of shade to rest and eat. It was sure nice to see familiar faces. All of us trudged up hill in misery together. Four women, all strangers yet becoming friends, hiking together. I've been told this is a rarity on trail (only women hiking together), but it can't be *that* rare if it happened with us in the first couple of weeks while on the PCT.

The winding PCT north of Scissors Crossing

The valley and the road leading into Warner Springs, when we can see it, is far down below now. I'm not sure how many feet we have climbed, but it looks significant (on an elevation profile map it's around 1200 feet. It seems higher to me).

Today ended up being hot and had absolutely NO water sources after the trailhead. I packed out five liters and found myself with a little over one left as I set up camp at mile 86.6 in a little saddle area between hills. The others pressed on after a break wanting to make at least 2 more miles. The next water source from where I'm setting up camp is a large water cache maintained by trail angels 5 miles further on trail called the "3rd Gate Water Cache". There's a series of three pipe gates to control livestock and the water catch is near the third pipe gate down a side trail. I really hope it's stocked when I get there tomorrow! I've heard it's reliable.

My camp spot is sheltered on a couple sides by a large brush and the hillside. Still, reports on Guthooks say that the area can get quite windy. I made 9 miles which was almost my goal for the day, but physically just 'bonked' out in the afternoon and had to stop early. This seems to be a theme for me, and I'm not sure why. Every afternoon, my energy just crashes. Even so, this is a great distance for being almost entirely uphill in the heat with a late start to the day. Maybe part of doing well was being well rested from my zero day? Two other hikers joined me an hour later and camped a fair distance away. This saddle has room for tons of tents and would be fantastic for a large trail family that likes to camp together.

***

Tonight, I'm really questioning exactly why I'm out here. Physically, my knees are swollen, and my toes are infected along with the normal aches and pains of hiking multiple hard miles during the day. I also torqued an ankle several times today but was saved from falling by my trusty trekking poles. Seriously, I know I avoided at least one face plant by halting my forward progress by slamming down my Lekis. I'm also moving so slow and realize that I will not make Canada at this rate before the weather window closes.

People who have successfully thru-hiked always say, "Never quit on a bad day." This isn't my first bad day on trail, plus I feel like I've had several in a row. This isn't *me*. I'm not a negative person and I can't figure out why I'm focusing in on the negative right now. I'm not having fun on the hike, especially when alone – I haven't had fun in days. This is also surprising since I normally do enjoy hiking alone, yet it was fantastic to share this experience with Chantel, Chris, and Betsy today. I want to keep up with them because I'm in such a better frame of mind when around them. My pace though… too slow.

There's no reason to be out here if I'm not enjoying myself. Maybe I will try section hiking? Ugh, I really don't want to give up on the thru-hike though. When I get to Warner Springs that will be the end of section "A" of

California on the PCT. I hadn't planned on going home until three or four days after that when reaching the Paradise Valley Café near mile 151, but think I need to go home at Warner Springs (mile 110) and get my head back in the game. At least get a good rest in and figure out what's going on with this old body of mine.

At the very least I can rest for a week and come back and do section B which ends a few miles past Interstate 10 (here after called the I-10 freeway) where I hiked over two days while training and testing gear last year. Maybe I can be a LASHer (Long Ass Section Hiker) instead of a thru hiker? If Tami will let me... she did say not to come home until I finished this thing. (Very Spartan of her – come back with your shield or on it.) Sorry hun, I think I'm too slow. First things first – two more days until Warner Springs.

***

The water I have left should last me through the night and tomorrow until I reach the water cache. No cooking tonight or tomorrow morning – only bars to eat as I must conserve the liter for drinking, not cooking.

Oh, I also noticed my clothing is fitting looser now. There must be some kind of weight loss happening. A welcome side effect of the long hours of hiking every day!

Emotionally, it's been a rough day. When times are good on trail, you don't dwell so much over how you miss your loved ones. When times are bad, you want nothing more than to be in their arms.

The wind is picking up now – hope I can sleep.

April 18th 2019

For once, I got a decent start today. A little after 7 AM, I had completely packed up and hiked out in an attempt to beat the heat of the day. Since the water supply is low, breakfast was a few bites of beef jerky. The plan is to get to the water cache and have a second breakfast of granola with rehydrated milk.

This morning I noticed my left foot hurting a great deal beyond the regular aches and pains that long hours of hiking bring on. It is making me 'gimpy' and I hope it manages to work itself out as I walk today. If it doesn't improve, I think I should see a foot doctor, or someone who can x-ray it to make sure there isn't anything serious going on when I'm closer to civilization.

The trail wound its way up, cholla and other types of cacti crowding the path all the way to the second pipe gate on this portion of the PCT. I think this is where Chantel and Chris planned to camp last night. They are long gone of course by this time – I know Chantel likes super early starts. Not sure about Chris though. There's a gorgeous view of the valley floor from this camp site, but I bet it was windy too as it looked pretty exposed without a lot of natural wind breaks.

Oooh – I witnessed a smack down wrestling match between a stink bug and caterpillar. Rolling right down the middle of the PCT as I gingerly stepped around the fracas. A few yards earlier I saw a stink bug chowing down on another bug of some sort. I never knew they were carnivorous. Yikes!

Leaving the knock-down fight behind me, I continued to climb on and off while the trail hugged ridgelines. Eventually I heard voices ahead, around a bend and nearly jumped for joy when I saw a pipe gate appear before me. This is the '3rd gate' which meant that the water cache was close, three tenths of a mile down a side trail off the PCT. The voices were familiar and who do my eyes see as I reached the junction to the cache, but Chantel and Chris. I also saw Tripod who I hadn't seen since the Fred Canyon campsite two days before Mt. Laguna. Tripod was given his name because he literally carries a tripod along with a large camera and lens to document the hike and scenery. I was happy to see them even though they were already preparing to hike on after refilling their water down below. The cache maintainers had placed a trail register at the junction of both trails for us to sign. I signed quickly and started shuffling down the side trail passing many shady camping sites. If you can make it here coming out of Scissors Crossing, this is a great place to stay. In a few minutes I met Betsy coming back up the trail from the water cache. The gang is all here! Well, for a few minutes. They were heading out momentarily. Oh well. I knew I needed to rest, rehydrate and make a real breakfast.

(Without this water, some hikers would have a difficult time making it between Scissors Crossing and Barrel Springs nearly 25 miles north. There are no natural sources, even in a wet year like this year. Thank you 3rd Gate Cache maintainers for all you do out of the kindness of your hearts.)

The 3rd gate water cache sign directing hikers to delicious water

Reaching the bottom of the path, a large water cache spread out before me. No one was there at that moment. A small "A" frame structure held empty gallon jugs and a small donation jar hung from one side to help the trail angels maintain the cache. Pallets and pallets of water sat partially shaded by brush and scruffy manzanita trees. I immediately got to work as soon as I dropped my backpack and started funneling water into my bottles. No need to filter here, so it was quick work. The water was cool too – a welcome surprise on an already warm morning. I sat down in the shade, kicked off my shoes drank delightful, chilled water and fixed some granola for breakfast. It was nice to cool off for a while. Eventually, a few other hikers I'd never met joined me at the cache before I started to pack up to make the ascent back up to the PCT. I wanted to dig a cat hole and attempt to… you know… answer the call of nature, but never felt like I could find a spot where I wouldn't be seen by hikers coming down the trail. It wasn't an emergency yet, so I gave up and left.

 The three tenths to the PCT was only the start of more climbing for quite some time; the trail hugged the hills and had great views. One of them included looking *straight* down to the water cache area. Yeah – my butt would have been hanging out for all to see if I tried to take care of business down there. Glad I skipped!

 A few hours later I started to scan the sides of the trail for a shady spot to have lunch. It was warm again. There isn't much shade, but I managed to find a small spot to fold myself into and eat. Far across the canyon, splashes of yellow color painted its walls from spring's desert flower bloom.

 You can find the most picturesque spots to rest on this trail.

 Lunch was over far too quickly. I jammed my swollen toes back into my shoes, hefted my pack and continued.

 Next, the PCT followed along ridges with sheer drops to one side. Call me weird, but I love this type of hiking, it's exciting. Finally, I crested the top of the San Felipe hills and could see civilization far in the distance. I think it's a mild trail from here to Barrel Springs situated a little past mile 101. Yes! Most of the uphill for the day is done. I can't tell you how happy I am about that. I wonder how far ahead Chantel, Chris and Betsy are?

I walked by a small cave and recognized it as "Billy Goat's" cave – a known milestone along this part of the trail. Billy Goat is a legendary hiker of the PCT and hikes it frequently. The cave is very small with a sandy bed, just large enough for one to sleep in, not necessarily tall enough to sit up in though. It was far too early for me to call it a day though, plus my goal was to make it to Barrel Springs tonight before camping. That will be a 16-mile day and would be my longest yet, but at least from this point forward (for a day or so), the trail promised to be gentle with mild ups and downs. An added bonus was a fabulous view of mountain sides to the north covered in orange poppies.

My left foot is really hurting, I can see a road down in the distance that might be the road at Barrel Springs. I don't know how busy the road is, but I think I need to get this foot looked at by a doctor as soon as possible. It's a weird pain that is beyond the usual aches and pains and is excruciating when I push off while walking. It will be late when I get there though, there are several camp spots down there too, with a water source. I'm just not sure what I'm going to do when I get there.

As the afternoon passes, I realize that I'm definitely going to hit my 16-mile goal today. It helps to have a smooth trail. It is well maintained at this point which makes it easy to make good time, even if I am limping. I think I'll make it to Barrel Springs by 5 PM, but I'm going to be dead on my feet when I get there, that's for sure. It sure is nice to feel like you're making good progress.

The trail swings around a bend and I am surprised by rocks spelling out "100". I made 100 miles on the PCT!

That's just crazy. I mean, I know I've been out here a while, but to think I walked 100 miles on varied terrain...

Not long after the 100 miles marker, I limped into Barrel Springs after hiking past oak trees and poison oak to each side of the trail. Water is near and changes the desert so much by its presence. It's a little after 5 PM, but I completed my longest day ever so far; 16 miles.

I glanced around and saw a few hikers setting up tents but continued toward the dirt parking lot along the road. I saw a small RV pulling out to leave. I bet that was Betsy. Her husband has been following her in a RV and supporting her at stops where he can drive the vehicle. It's a nice set up and allows her to have a soft bed outside of trail towns. There is a mountain yogi retreat a little more than a mile down the road where they are probably headed. I'm thinking about going there but want to try to get a ride home first to get this foot checked out. The yogi center, named Mountain Valley Retreat, has very limited space for hikers, so I figured they are probably full anyway.

I see another car in the lot with a chair set out and cooler next to it. A man stood talking to Chantel and Tripod, handing out sodas and chips. Trail magic! Finally, I was in time to experience it. Chantel turned around and cheered. I laughed, temporarily forgetting my foot and gladly accepted a soda. That was one of the best Cokes I've had in my life. Chantel let me know that the RV was indeed Betsy and hubby heading out and that Chris was back in the camp area probably setting up her tent or filtering water.

Even with this uplifting experience, I knew I had to exit the trail and get my foot checked out. My fear is that I developed a stress fracture, but I honestly didn't know for sure what was going on, only that it hurt. A lot. I had cell service, so I tried to call an Uber or Lyft without luck. My home is about two hours from here and no doubt will be an expensive ride, yet I had a singular mission to go regardless. I did not have any luck though. Apparently, the area was too remote for any drivers to get or accept a 'ping'. Instead, I gave the Yogi center a call to see if they had room for one more hiker and asked the trail angel if he would mind giving me a lift there. Tripod wanted to go too. I talked to the owner and even though it was nearly dark at that time, she said she had room. It costs to stay there, but a nominal amount. If you are in distress, it's a phenomenal place to recoup. I still didn't have a ride home, but I think I can come up with a plan in the morning or even convince Tami to come get me. If I can't get a ride all the way home at least I could get myself closer to make it easier for Tami to pick me up. The Paradise Valley Café 50+ miles further up the trail would be the best area to find a ride. We will see.

  The Mountain Valley Retreat is a nice place in the backcountry about 1.5 miles from Barrel Springs nestled in green area with tall oaks and set on a large property. There are all sorts of services you can purchase from them and classes to take, but I was there for rest. The owner can accommodate up to ten hikers and has a bunkhouse and a few teepees on the lot for people to stay in. There is a common room for us to sit and relax with an attached laundry room and a shower and a couple of restrooms. By the time Tripod and I arrived it was pitch black. We stumbled around with our headlamps on, trying to find our way to the bunkhouse. I saw Betsy's RV in the driveway, lights out, already asleep.

  After the unplanned, after dark tour of the grounds, Tripod and I finally found the bunkhouse, dropped our bags and enjoyed the common area for a while. He took a never-ending shower, while I soaked my feet in Epsom salts. There were two other beat-up hikers there also. I couldn't resist the allure of a wash too, so I had a delicious shower (thank goodness Tripod hadn't used up all the hot water). Soon afterward, the long mile day was catching up and my feet didn't feel much better, so called it a night was the first to crawl into my bunk.

April 19, 2019

There are three friendly cats at the retreat, two of which love as much attention as possible. They received lots of it this morning from me.

I think Betsy was surprised to see me when she climbed out of their RV with her husband to join the rest of us for breakfast this morning. The owner cooks and prepares a wonderful breakfast for a modest amount of money at the retreat. Well worth it in my opinion. At breakfast, Betsy's hubby offered to take me up to the Paradise Valley Café after he investigated a road past Warner Springs. (This was a narrow road that led to a nearby trailhead Betsy could take to spend a night in the RV between Warner Springs and Highway 74 a few days further along the PCT.)

After breakfast, Tripod joined us when it was time to pile into the RV and Betsy's hubby drove to Barrel Springs and dropped them off. Overwhelmingly, I felt depressed watching them go and regretted not going with them but knew my foot wouldn't support me the entire 8+ miles into Warner Springs. Fast forward a few hours later, I was sitting at the Paradise Valley Café having lunch and waiting for Tami to drive up from the desert where we live to take me home. Most of the hikers at the café I had never seen before except for a couple of Germans who started the same day I had. Dang – some people are so fast! That means, by that point, they were three or four days ahead of me.

Tami pulled up to the Café and was not happy with me. Again, think of a Spartan wife who would tell their sons to "Come back with your shield or on it" and you'll get the idea. I had talked nonstop about the trail since meeting her, and now, on the year where I was to finally attempt it, I was coming home earlier than planned. Possibly out for good. There was also a lot of personal sacrifice made in order to get me on trail (time off not used for mutual vacation and funds) as well. Not to mention the emotional toll it takes because of the separation. I was pleased to see her but kept silent for most of the drive home because she was not in the mood to talk.

We rolled home shortly before 5 PM and I immediately got on the phone to call the foot doctor and make an appointment as soon as possible to see what was wrong with my left foot. Surprisingly, I was able to get an appointment set for Monday morning. In the meantime, I planned on resting it and getting the toes as clean as possible. I still don't have any blisters, but the ingrown toenails are gross and one turning black. Eventually, I'm no doubt going to lose that toenail.

If it's a soft tissue injury, I want to get back out and finish section A and at least part of B of the PCT. I think if I feel good, I'll keep going and complete section B which ends a little past the I-10 freeway.

I'm so happy, yet sad to be home. It's killing me to not be hiking with the new friends I made on trail… whether or not I can keep up with them at this point. I guess it's just the way it has to be. Maybe they'll take a lot of time off in Idyllwild, the next town near the trail, and I can catch up? Who knows?

Chapter Five
Home and Back again

April 22nd 2019

The foot is feeling a little better since resting after getting but still not normal by any means. I headed out to see the doctor this morning not knowing what to expect. My podiatrist took an X-Ray of my left foot and the good news was that I didn't have a stress fracture. However, he did say the foot had severe arthritis and the swelling experienced during the thru hike was compounding the problem. I knew I had arthritis, heck I deal with mild rheumatoid arthritis too, but I didn't think it would impact the hike as much as it currently is.

I take Turmeric and Ibuprofen (or as hikers call it, "Vitamin I") to help control inflammation, but the foot doctor said that wasn't enough to alleviate the extra pressure and swelling on the arthritic joints. The pain would only get worse over time if the joint stayed swollen. He gave me a prescription for Meloxicam, an anti-inflammatory that seems to do better with arthritis than Ibuprofen. The pills help but has some bad side effects that are not good for hiking long distances without frequent pit toilets along the way! I will take it here at home, but when I get back on trail I will rely on turmeric and vitamin I for now. The doctor also wanted me to ice my foot at the end of every day on trail. Um… yeah, not going to be possible. I'm not sure he understands what hiking a long trail is and how remote it can be.

Plans to get back on trail ASAP have hit a snag. I really want to finish section A at the very least and possibly continue on through section B. However, Tami can't drive me back to Barrel Springs, where I left off a few days ago. There's a trail angel, Joni, in the valley where I live who offered before I started this adventure to give me a ride if I needed one. I reached out to her today and she said she said she can drive me back to the trail this Saturday. That's so awesome of her, I can't wait to meet her in person and get back on the PCT.

I'll also have four more full days to rest my foot – I'm going to lose my trail legs by Saturday though. Oh well, I technically don't have those perfect trail legs yet, but I will lose any progress that I've made with my hiking fitness. At least the miles between Barrel and Warner Springs look mild, a good part to warm the legs back up.

April 27th, 2019

On my way back to the trail! Two local trail angels that watch my videos offered to take me back to where I'd left off, so I wouldn't miss an inch of the trail. This is no small thing, it's about a two-hour drive from the Coachella Valley to Barrel Springs. Thank you, Joni and Elizabeth, from the bottom of my heart for getting me where I needed to go. They said a quiet prayer for me before I left. I'm not a religious person, but it was appreciated. Especially as I need all the help I can get.

It is forecast to be warm today but so far it isn't too bad. The goal for the day is to reach Warner Springs a bit over 8 miles up the trail. The elevation profile doesn't look horrible – some of your typical ups and downs but mild gain and loss. The first thing I walked into was a grassy area with tall oaks before heading up and over small ridges with meadows on the side. It's definitely a lot greener in this part than south of Barrel Springs. Up on the ridge, a forest of yucca plants guided the way. Far away, on the opposite side of the valley, I can also still see a large splash of orange, poppies painting the walls to the north.

I took a deep breath. It's so nice to be back on the trail.

At the beginning of a small meadow that the trail crossed, I found a small shady area to hide from the sun and eat lunch. The view spanned the small meadow and the trail winding its way up and over the hill on the other side. A wooden post stood in the middle of it with "PCT" carved vertically into its sides.

Some of the photography tools I brought along enable me to get a little creative if no other hikers are around to take a video or photo of me on trail. (I'd feel a bit silly with others around.) I carry a small, bendable tripod which you can wrap around posts, signs, etc. I also have a small Bluetooth 'clicker' that will take photos for you from a distance as long as it's synced to your camera. I primarily shoot footage with my phone camera and carry a lightweight mount that can be fastened to the tripod or a device you can attach onto the end of your trekking poles (think of a large selfie stick).

After I finishing lunch, I walked to the wooden PCT post and affixed the tripod with phone pointing up the trail and had some fun taking stills and short video clips of me hiking away. It takes a few minutes to set up special shots like that – and that makes a slow hiker like me even slower – but the memories saved are well worth it.

Author walking through the first of many gorgeous meadows

Now, making it over another hill, I see an even larger meadow the PCT cuts a visible line through. The trail is so varied today and beautiful. You hike along little ridges, not too steep and not for long and then you come to a wooded glen which is followed by more climbing and then bam – into wonderful meadows.

The wind has made its reappearance and creates ripples along the tips of the meadow grasses generating green and purple waves. If there was water, I could well imagine I was at a strange technicolor beach. From what I've been told, this area usually contains lots of cows grazing on the tall grass, but sadly there are none to be seen today.

Hiking into the large meadow with old wooden PCT signpost

The dandelions out here are bizarre. They are not the fragile, white puff balls that I grew up seeing – instead they are a spiky metallic silver that looks like they could do harm. What kind of wishes would these spikes grant if blown apart?

I dropped into a sheltered area, the trail returning to trees in a small ravine and a flowing San Ysidro Creek. The PCT travels alongside the water for a short while and many a hiker reclined in the shade enjoying the cool water from the creek. Some were completely passed out taking well deserved naps. I found a spot right along the water to snack and rest. There are several tent sites near this area too. I want to soak my feet in the water but don't want to pollute it for those filling up further downstream. That's just gross. Instead, I scooped up water using my CNOC bladder and filtered it into liter bottles. I haven't kept any water permanently in the bladder so far, I've only used it as a way to gather water easily for filtering. This should be the last time I need to grab water before I reach Warner Springs where I look forward to soaking my feet.

The PCT makes a sharp turn away from San Ysidro Creek and zig zags up quickly to another meadow with boulder formations in the distance. I stood gazing into the distance...I think I can identify Eagle Rock from here but am not sure. The formation sits about a mile from the creek and from one angle resembles a standing eagle, spreading its wings while looking to its left. I've seen it in lots of videos and photos, a major landmark along the trail and close enough to Warner Springs for many day hikers to visit it too. I can't wait to see it in person.

Poppies dot the landscape, in fact there are a *lot* around me right now. I suddenly feel very sleepy...

After a peaceful stroll through the meadow, I took the short spur trail up to Eagle Rock. And yes, from one side it looks just like it was described. I convinced some day hikers to take a few photos of me if I could haul my old carcass on top of the formation. Hilarity ensued as I wobbled my way up to the 'shoulder' of its wing. I wanted to sit on its head but didn't feel confident in my rock scrambling skills at that moment. Instead, I stood along its wing and struck a warrior pose with my trekking poles. The pictures the hikers took were epic! A couple thru-hikers from Australia climbed the boulders after I shimmied down, carrying a didgeridoo and played it from the top of the eagle. Both moments, mine and theirs, felt powerful – the trail and the naturally formed monument giving blessings to our adventure in the wild.

Author striking a warrior pose on Eagle Rock

    The meadow became greener the closer to Warner Springs the trail got, more water making an appearance. The last few miles follow a creek all the way to town – very nice to hike in dappled shade. I was having a great time except my feet have flared up again and are hurting quite a bit. Both feet this time, not just the left. Huge oak trees grew here and there near the creek. If you've ever seen "Something Wicked This Way Comes", they looked exactly like *that* tree. Amazing, beautiful… and a little creepy too.

Woods south of Warner Springs, CA

Distant road noise interrupted the solitude of the trail as the miles ticked down. Warner Springs must be close. This has been one of my favorite sections of the trail to hike. Lots of neat landmarks and variety over these 8+ miles.

I came across a sign directing hikers to take a spur trail to get to the post office in town, but it's Saturday afternoon and I know it's closed already so I can't pick up my resupply until Monday. For now, I will continue on the PCT and go to the community center in town. I need to get off these feet, they are killing me.

The Warner Springs Community Center has set aside a small bit of land next to the high school to allow thru hikers to pitch tents free of charge (although they do run on donations). They have flush toilets for our use and a small building where they provide services and sell resupply. They're limited to what they can carry, but if you've forgotten to send yourself something, they will probably have what you need. They also provide buckets of water and soap (for a small fee) that you can use to do laundry or take a shower using a bucket. Yes, "Bucket Showers". Also, an outfitter that operates out of a large RV/5th wheel is allowed to operate there and sell gear to hikers. By the time hikers reach Warner Springs at miles 110ish, many decide to change up their gear somewhat and having an outfitter there is *very* useful.

Because it was a weekend, there were locals that had time to offer rides between the resource center and Ranch Resort a mile down the highway. The Warner Springs Ranch Resort has a restaurant that sits on a golf course across the highway from cottages you can rent rooms in. I ate dinner there – great food, but it took forever to get the order. Too many hungry mouths and not enough help, I think. While there, I only ever saw two waitresses working several tables. Near the restaurant is also a gas station/convenience store and the post office is one door down the highway.

After stuffing my face and hanging out with other beat hikers, I grabbed a ride back to the resource center and set up my tent a bit away from the tree hoping to avoid snoring and other noises that might keep me up. There was a family next to me, grandparents with two of their grandchildren from Yuma, who watched my channel on YouTube and recognized me. That's kind of a weird feeling, I have to admit, I'll never quite get used to it. They were very nice though and were awesome to camp next too.

Also nearby were some picnic tables with a canopy overhead which some hikers congregated by well past 'hiker midnight'.

Sigh.

Well, since I can't sleep, I think I'll edit a video and catch up on my journal writing while waiting for them to call it a night.

I must 'zero' here tomorrow in order to wait for Monday so I can pick up my resupply package from the post office. My feet feel a little better since I've been in recovery flip flops and out of hiking shoes after reaching town. All in all, this was a great hike to welcome me back to the PCT.

April 28th, 2019

Zero day in Warner Springs. A forced zero day in order to get my resupply package at the post office as mentioned before... it's Sunday.

Considering the number of hikers there last night, I was able to get a good night's sleep. This was the first time my tent had an issue with condensation though. I couldn't figure out why until another hiker mentioned that camping on grass causes most tents to have that problem. I'll have to drape my sleeping quilt out to dry at some point this morning when it warms up. Wild turkeys serenaded me as I crawled out of the tent to make an early morning trip to the restroom. I couldn't see them anywhere, but I could hear the gobbles coming from the field and trees not too far away.

Later that morning, I had some breakfast, chatted with the family from Yuma and soaked my feet at the center in warm water and Epsom salts. The center had three large 'hiker boxes' filled with clothing, food and various other items used during a thru hike. I always look through them and frequently leave extra food that I know I won't need during the next leg. There were some goofy things in the boxes this time around that I had a hard time believing that anyone packed for the hike – for instance styling paste for one's hair. Why??? I found a large tube of Aspercreme which I could use but there was no way I was going to carry that huge thing around. Too much weight. I wish it was a sample size tube.

Next, I visited 2-foot Adventures in their silver trailer they had set up next to the center. They do a brisk business with hikers switching out gear after learning over 100+ miles what works and what doesn't during the hike. After poking my head inside to check out the merchandise, decided I didn't need anything just yet. Although, if they had a Big Agnes Tiger Wall tent, I would have been tempted to replace my Copper Spur that day. They did not.

For my second day in Warner Springs I wanted to stay in one of the newly opened cottage rooms at the old resort. They are decently priced, and I wanted to get away from the noise of the camping area near the center. The resort has fallen on bad times and new owners are trying to rebuild what it once was years ago. Because of this, not all amenities have reopened and the price to stay isn't exorbitant. There is nothing to do in Warner Springs so there's a lot of downtime. If I wasn't waiting for my resupply box from the post office, it would be better to hike out. (In hindsight, I should have.) As it was, I waited for what seemed like forever to be allowed to check in at the resort. Once I was able to get a key, I made a beeline to my room, tossed my pack down and looked forward to getting a warm shower.

The cottages are rustic with adobe walls on the inside. No TV, no radio. The bathrooms are up to date, but I found tiny spiders in my bath towel. Eeek! There's a reason why I haven't cowboy camped yet – all the creepy crawlies of the desert. I'm very phobic when it comes to spiders. This was not a good start to my shower! I flung the first towel into a distance corner of the restroom thinking this would keep the spiders from me. Twitching, I unfolded the next towel which seemed to be arachnid free. Even so, I shook it out before using it.

Skin stung on my fingers and thumbs as I washed the filth away. My skin is splitting along the tips and joints in many places. The water I've been guzzling does not seem to help keep my skin hydrated. My hiking clothes aren't that dirty yet. I'll sink wash my extra pair of socks and undies and let them dry while I head across the street to grab dinner again tonight at the restaurant. I think this time I'll order a pizza so I will have enough left over for breakfast in the morning and get hiking as soon as possible.

The plan for tomorrow is to get up early, pick up my resupply box at the post office when it opens, organize my food back in the room and check out soon afterward. Next, I'll have to hike an extra mile back to the trailhead at the resource center. It's supposed to rain tomorrow. Hopefully not, but I have a pack cover and rain jacket so I should be fine even if it does rain.

April 29th, 2019

Drizzle chased me across the street to the post office which isn't open yet, but the front doors were unlocked, letting me escape the elements and wait under cover until 9 AM. There were two hiker boxes inside too, packed with oatmeal among other things. Discarded oatmeal is a theme so far in all hiker boxes. I don't care for it, so I leave any packets I see in the boxes. Someone who likes the stuff will eventually snag it. I was the first customer this morning, got my box and took it back to the cottage room to get everything organized in my food bag. One thing I'm getting better at is emptying food out of packaging and condensing it into Ziploc bags. Any chips? Every bag gets poured into one large Ziploc. Candy? Also poured into their own specific bag. At times I'll even do this with granola bars if they don't have chocolate (which melts all over if not in its wrapper).

When it was time for me to check out of the cottage and head out to take the mile access trail back to the resource center it began to rain. The PCT continues near the resource center where I left off on Saturday. The rain increased and pelted me through my rain gear. I had a pack cover on and a rain jacket, yet I could feel the water seeping between my back and the backpack. Half a mile later, I could feel the water wetting through my jacket. It wasn't an old rain jacket,

I think I'd had it a year, but it failed, and I was getting soaked. I really hope the rain doesn't get worse today. I have dry sacks inside my pack, but water is still getting through to the inside and I'm afraid of my down gear getting wet. (Gear that is made of 'down', or feathers, is not waterproof and loses its insulation properties when it gets wet.) I know my puffy must be soaked as I didn't stick it in a dry sack. When I reach the center, I'll try to check things out. We can't bring our packs inside as there's just not enough room, so I must wait until there's a break in the weather to examine what's happened in my bag.

The march in the wetness continued, rain coming down relentlessly as I finally reached the outer fields of the school. I hustled as fast as I could to reach cover.

After dropping off my wet pack on the stoop outside of the resource center under the front awning, I slogged inside to find it packed with hikers escaping the rain. When I was warm enough, I went back outside and checked through my bag finding my down gear wet – especially my puffy jacket. It was completely soaked through and useless. Torrential rain was predicted for the rest of the day, so I'm not sure what to do as that jacket is part of my sleep layer as well.

***

I must take a step back here and explain why this freaked me out so much at the time. I mentioned this experience briefly earlier. While I was training for the PCT, I participated in an overnight campout with two other future 2019 PCT hikers (Turtle and Skyscraper) at the White Water Preserve. Rain was predicted that night, so we thought it would be a great opportunity to try out our sleep gear and tents after a short hike. I did not have any dry sacks at the time, just a pack cover and jacket. We were all wet by the time we crawled into our tents after a brief dinner. Hours later I found I could not retain any warmth and began shaking violently. The rain was pouring down, it had been pelting from the sky for hours. My down was a little wet, but I do not recall it being soaked through – it was just bitingly cold, and I knew I was in trouble if I didn't get under better cover. I threw on my rain jacket and shoes, made a run with as much gear as possible to toss into my car, ran back to break down as much of the tent as I could and drag everything to my Honda. Hunkering down in my car, I tried to warm up having mixed success (I was thinking of trying to sleep in the car, but I still couldn't get warm without turning it on and running the heater, plus sleeping in a civic is not comfortable for a 5'11" frame). All of us lived within an hour or so from the preserve, so even though it was late, I decided to call it and throw in the proverbial towel for the night. Before leaving I stumbled out of the car and made my way back to where Turtle and Skyscraper's tent was pitched to let them know I was bailing out. They were having problems too and left a couple hours after I did. Really a 'wash' of a night, but I learned a few things about keeping warm in less than ideal circumstances.

***

    Remembering that experience while at Warner Springs made me lose the 'mental battle' against the pitfalls the PCT throws at you. I knew I couldn't go out and hike today, that was certain. My biggest fear was that my down was ruined, and I couldn't get it dry to sleep in tonight in the tent. The puffy was a goner unless it was possible to wash it and dry it in such a way to regain its loft. I thought about walking back to the cottages to see if one was available again tonight but figured everyone else already had that idea and they were more than likely sold out. (They were.)
    Mentally, emotionally, I just want to go home. (Stressing out just a little bit.) Home was over two hours away though by car. With equipment/clothing out of commission, I have decided to call it and try to get a ride

home. Here's the problem though, Warner Springs is in the middle of nowhere, like Barrel Springs, and hard to get a ride anywhere, let alone home. If I can resuscitate the down at home, I may try to come back and knock out another section of the trail this season. If not, I can 'trail angel' by the I-10 where the trail crosses underneath on its way into the San Gorgonio wilderness. Another option is skipping ahead and hit other sections of the trail, but I like a good linear hike, so I probably won't do that.

Shivering every time I stepped outside of the resource center, I bought a Gatorade inside and huddled next to other hikers trying to think of my next move. It is *so* cold outside. The cold doesn't bother me as much when I have dry gear. In fact, if the weather was constantly this cool, but without precipitation, it would be perfect hiking weather for me.

The people at the center are extremely helpful. Although there was no Uber/Lyft/Taxi service in the area, the lady working the front of the center said that there was a local that gave rides as far as a few hours away for a fee. I gave him a call and he agreed to come get me and transport me back to the Coachella Valley after his doctor's appointment that day. I took the two hours to dry off completely inside and nibbled on the food I resupplied with this morning. A large portion of the box I picked up this morning at the post office ended up in the center's hiker box. I knew someone could use the food and it would not go to waste. A large jigsaw puzzle of the PCT sat on a table in the center which I took apart and started again. Several other hikers joined me, all keeping warm hiding from the storm outside. The ride arrived eventually, I piled in with my soaking wet pack and settled in for the long, sad ride home.

**

In hindsight, I should have just sucked it up and stayed and dealt with the cold and wetness. One problem, well more of a weakness for me, is that sections A, B and C are all close to home. Too much so, because it gives me an easy way to bail out of the hike when there is a little bit of trouble I don't believe I can handle. If I didn't have that safety net, who knows what I would have done – I would be forced to deal with the problems more rather than hitting the panic switch and going home immediately.

***

When I got home, I unpacked my gear and scattered it all over the garage to dry, pieces of the tent hanging from the rafters, my sleep layer draped across a card table and chair. Clothing bits flung across cabinets. Everything, everywhere. The puffy jacket and backpack were really soaked. I have some down cleaner and a plastic ball that you toss in the drier with the jacket to help recover the loft of the feathers inside. I hope that this can 'revive' the down so I can use it in the future. Next, I pulled out the dry sacks I had my sleep layer and the down quilt stored in. The quilt was a little wet, but not nearly as badly as I had feared. The sleep layer was a little damp but overall, pretty dry. I could kick myself right now because I think that I may have been OK hunkering down for one more night and taking another zero day. I mean, it would have been cold, and I may not have slept much, but if the following day was sunny at all I could have dried out most of my gear before continuing north. Mentally though, I just wanted to leave the trail. The only drawback in the condition my gear ended up being, was that I would be short a jacket that was a key component of my warmth system. I slept in that *every* night and it kept me warm in camp as well. Then again, there was always 2-foot adventures to find a new layer to buy if they carried my size.

I'm thinking about going back again this weekend to continue, but emotionally my partner is having trouble dealing with my constant back and forth. It was taking its toll on her too, not just me. This is one subject I don't see talked about very often in writing, in social media or vlogs very often. What happens to those you leave behind when you attempt something like a thru-hike on a long trail like the Pacific Crest Trail? Some people are lucky and have a friend or family member that has done a hike like this before and others around him/her understand what the sacrifice is for both the hiker and support person. Emotionally, physically and financially. Most people will not have this luxury. Then there is the rare breed that can do the entire hike solo without a support person at home. They generally are super self-reliant, take the extra time to mail themselves resupply boxes *while* hiking on trail, or roll the dice and live off the hiker box leavings and the goodness of others. Yet, for those of us who have people at home who love, miss and worry about you while in the wild, the happiness to see you when you get home can be wonderful while leaving tears them apart. I've done this twice now… I don't quite know what to say.

***

Also, today I find myself questioning my mode of solo hiking. Should I have tried to hike faster and hike with friends or would that have resulted in an injury? Friends that I knew prior to beginning the PCT started a few weeks earlier than me. Should I have started earlier and hiked with them? Would I have done better under either circumstance? Would they have talked sense into me when I made up my mind to get off trail?

Chapter Six
One Last Try

May 18, 2019

  Bryan, Tami's son, came home from college recently and after some prodding, she offered to take me back out to the trail if I still wanted to go because she would now not be alone at home while I hiked. At this point, I only want to hike the first half of Section B which runs from Warner Springs to approximately the Paradise Valley Café area of the PCT. The actual trail crosses Highway 74 about a mile from the café but is a good stopping point before you climb ever higher in elevation and eventually around the shoulder of Mt. San Jacinto.
  This morning we all set out in Tami's car to Warner Springs where they dropped me off at the resource center. After a quick restroom break, I picked up where I left off along the trail. After a mere five minutes on the trail a bug flew up my nose. Yuck!
  My goal is the Paradise Valley Café in three or four days. Today is nice, but rain is forecast for tomorrow. I changed up my gear a bit while at home, so I *should* be OK. First, I ditched the puffy and am going with a pull over fleece instead. Fleece isn't waterproof of course but isn't

completely useless if it does get rained on. Next, I dropped my pack cover and added a poncho designed to be worn over yourself and a pack. Also, since my rain jacket wetted out, I decided to use a smaller size jacket – an Outdoor Research (OR) Helium Hybrid as my new shell. It fits snug, but hopefully will keep the water away from me when not using the poncho.

The first few miles were more of Warner Springs' gorgeous meadows and so far, the weather is lovely, sunny and cool. High winds are forecast for tomorrow along with rain, but I should be at Mike's place (a trail angel that has a place less than a mile off the trail) by the afternoon. He has some buildings there that I could hunker down behind and use as a wind break if needed. I've never actually been there, so I don't know exactly what to expect.

Pipe gate north of Warner Springs that has seen better days

There is a small airport near Warner Springs where you can pay to take glider rides. One lazily flew over me while hiking through the meadow. I had seen these before, flying around near the trail in April.

The trail changed from meadowland to shaded glens with oak trees and a challenge course to either side. There's a military training area nearby and I believe they use part of the trail and campground nearby for exercise. I knew that I was getting nearer to Agua Caliente Creek. Highway 79 sits above the lowest part of the creek and the PCT runs underneath the bridge prior to traveling alongside the water before the path begins to climb. This will be the first crossing of *many* for this creek. It smells strongly of sulfur near the bridge. Phew – that stink!

I came across another campground, this one with an open wooden shack sitting in the middle. Not sure what the building's purpose was for, but I recognized it from another YouTube vlogger hiking this year named Second Chance Hiker. A couple of months ago when he hiked through the area, he found the shack packed with trash. As a result, he challenged the rest of the class of 2019 thru-hikers to take a few pieces of trash and pack it out as he was doing, to help clean it up. It's now completely clean. "Yay!" Our class rose to the occasion! Either that or a good Samaritan hiked up and packed it all out. Either way, great job class of 2019.

(If you get the chance, look up Second Chance Hiker on YouTube. This man was on a mission and did well. His journey continues.)

Wandering through fallen leaves, I sat down under a large tree 25 yards from the shack and took a lengthy lunch break. This is one thing I believe I neglected until now, I rarely took a long break to eat and rest during the day with the need for miles pressing down on my head. I think this was an incorrect mindset and know that resting when shade is to be had is a good idea for my body.

From my shady lunch spot, the trail seemed to be going uphill at all times. This felt harder than the first day of hiking back in April. It is not hot, but I've definitely lost my trail legs by being home. Physically, today is very tough. The colors are still here though. The prickly pear cacti are now blossoming with deep, pink flowers splashing colors amongst the browns and greens. The snakes are still out and about. I walked around a turn on the trail and a snake vacated the path where my foot was about to land. Scared the crap out of me! It was not a rattle snake but probably a garter snake – black with yellow racing stripes. I think I scared it as much as it did me.

After putting my heart back into my chest, I continued uphill… plodding slower and slower as the day went on. Today is starting to take its toll and I'm beginning to feel queasy. It is delicious when I come across the rare downhill or flat part of the trail that lets one set of muscles rest for a short while.

At one of the crossings of the creek I ended up taking my shoes off to cross, barefooting it across the cool water. The water felt great on my achy arthritic feet, the only downside was having to sit and clean the sand off before putting shoes and socks back on. Sand on feet equals an easy path to blisters. Especially when sand remains between toes.

Most of the creek crossings before this one could be done by hopping rocks or wading through very shallow portions of the stream bed. At one of the last crossings, I filled up my water bottles to capacity (four liters) and now will just push miles until time to make camp. It will be a 'dry' camp as the next source of reliable water won't be reached until tomorrow morning. There is one last camp spot coming up where the creek crosses near the trail one final time, but I will get there too early in the afternoon to justify stopping. The problem is that there is a long climb after that spot which I generally like to do in the morning when my legs are fresher. However, I want to get as far as possible today because of rain forecast for tomorrow.

Many of the plants near this area had a long orange growth which I found out later is called "Witches Hair".

There were clusters of this all over the trail and from a great distance could be mistaken for large poppy fields. Witches Hair is a moss or parasitic plant also called 'Dodder' and feeds off the host plant. I don't think it kills the host plant but sustains itself off of it until the dodder eventually dies off.

One feature I will need to look for tonight in a campsite is wind shelter to protect against sideways rain. I passed up a couple of exposed spots before finding a small area with tall chaparral and manzanita trees along the trail and surrounding a few level areas for tents. I picked the spot right next to the trail. There was enough room for two more tents behind a thin screen of brush, but no one else came by that evening after I set up my tent. Yet again a solo camp spot.

I made it roughly 8 miles today and am trying to eat dinner. The key word is 'trying'. I feel nauseous and nothing sounds good enough to try to eat. The only thing I have in my food bag that sounds palatable to my stomach is ramen. I broke off a little more than half a block of the ramen and tossed it in the cooking pot with some beef jerky and seasoning to cook. It tastes good but I'm even having trouble keeping this down.

Honestly, I'm not sure what to do. Mike's place is approximately 10 miles further up trail… and at least half of that is a steep elevation gain, which we all know by now I don't do well on the best of days, let alone sick. I do better with uphill slogs first thing in the morning after resting and eating, but I'm having trouble eating at this point too. The other option is to hike back down to Warner Springs. If I feel as bad as I do right now in the morning, I'm going to have to hike back down even though it's the last thing I *want* to do. The forecast calls for steady rain and there are a lot of creek crossings to do again if I decide to slog the 8 miles back south. I doubt they'll turn into raging rivers, but they'll be a bit more challenging than they were today to cross.

Section B so far is beating me… badly.
Whipping my arse.
Kicking my butt.

Soundly defeating me...
You get the picture.

May 19th, 2019

 A little past 1 AM: I've lost most of my dinner in a bush near the tent. Just great.
 3 AM-ish: Rain is coming down hard outside the tent. I'm managing to stay dry inside. I checked the weather forecast on my Garmin and saw a brief lull in the weather predicted between 5 AM and 7 AM. That's probably the best time to pack up camp. In the meantime, I have to try to rest. I'm leaning towards hiking back down to Warner Springs since I was unable to keep dinner in my stomach. Right now, breakfast doesn't sound good either. We will see if I can eat anything in a couple of hours.
 I woke up again around 6 AM. Other than being sick and the rain pouring down, I slept well. The campsite was indeed a good one that protected my tent from winds.
 Breakfast – nothing sounds palatable right now. I don't think I could stomach my granola and milk... the thought of milk makes my stomach churn. Granola with water doesn't sound good either. Maybe I'll eat more of the cliff bar I couldn't finish yesterday? That sounds a bit heavy though. Heck, I could have potato chips for breakfast – the salt sounds good. Ahhh, the diet of a long-distance hiker. Ridiculous!
 I still don't feel well and decide not to attempt the 10 miles to Mike's place. The elevation gain and predicted rain showers plus being sick... if I wasn't ill, I'd attempt it, but instead I'm going to hike back out after I send a text to Tami. It's still a long 8 miles, through rain. She answered, asking me to text back later to let her know when I was within a

couple miles of the Resource Center and she would start out from home at that point as it would take one – two hours in my condition to finish that last stretch.

As predicted, there was a lull in the rain, and I crawled out of the tent and began breaking everything down and packing as fast as I could. Of course, the rain fly on the tent was soaking as well as the ground sheet. There was no way to dry it before heading out, I dried what I could with a camp towel and stuffed them in a sack before slipping them into the backpack. Sprinkles started falling as I set out southbound back toward Warner Springs. I wouldn't be able to film much of the way back using the phone if the rain came down any harder.

After the first couple of miles I was already dead on my feet. The rain sure has made the desert green, but today's downpour is also making me miserable after racing to break down camp and toss the rain poncho on. The rain prevented me from pulling out my phone to take footage for the vlog and never stopped the entire day. The poncho is sort of working but I can tell my pack is still getting wet on the sides. I'm not sure how though, it all should be covered. Creek crossings are more challenging to cross because of the wet weather and the overgrown brush reaches out to dry its leaves and branches all over *me*. My legs and feet are soaked through. I need to stop and rest but know I would become too cold, so I instead press on.

The campground near Highway 79 was quiet and its giant trees blocked much of the rain. Wet and fatigued I leaned against a pole used for hanging food. I couldn't stop for too long as the chill of the day begins to creep in when stopping… but I was so tired. Away to my right I heard something stepping through the brush and look up to see a mother turkey with her chicks strutting through the campground. Soon after, I spied another flock ahead of me with even more chicks. So cute! Their adorableness takes my mind off the wet misery as I continue toward the underpass of the highway this will be my first real break of the day, sheltering from the rain.

Finally! I see the underpass and almost leap over the last crossing of the creek in my haste to get under cover. I plopped my backpack on a cement slab and peeled off rain gear to discover one half of my pack was actually not covered and now soaking wet, adding to its weight... on one side only. Argh! Apparently, I can't dress myself properly and the poncho was not covering the right side of the pack. Shrugging, I transferred some weight around and vowed that for the last few miles I would leave the left side of the pack uncovered if the poncho didn't fit completely around and even out the weight for my shoulders. My glasses fog up while resting underneath the bridge as I became chilly due to lack of movement. It is really cold when you're not moving.

I texted Tami to let her know I was an hour or so from the resource center so she could time her drive to pick me up. Wretched and grumpy, I wanted to avoid hiking those last few miles, so I clambered up the hillside to a shoulder of Highway 79 and tried hitching to the post office or restaurant a mile up the road. Highway 79 has very little shoulder most of the way and is unsafe to walk along, otherwise I would have considered road walking there instead. I had absolutely no luck flagging down a ride in the fifteen minutes I was above the trail. It could be no one wanted to stop in that weather for a homeless looking hiker wearing a giant green Frogg Togg poncho. Total hitchhiking 'fail'. I decided not to waste any more time and scooted back down the embankment to the trail and start the slog southbound to the resource center.

I saw one person during the last 2 miles starting their northbound hike for the day. At least there are some nice established campsites for him to stop at when he wants to stop.

After what seems like forever, I finally tottered to the center, dropped my pack under the eaves and made a beeline for the restroom. Ahhhh! I didn't realize it is a heated restroom until today. Next, I shuffled into the center to attempt to dry off and warm up. One of the volunteers remembered me and said I made a good call coming back down as it was now sleeting outside.

What?!

I peered out of the window and sure enough, sleet. She stated that they were expecting snow that night.

Yeah, I made the right call bailing out. Facing that weather when healthy is bad enough, facing it while you can't eat and keep it down is another story. I did a mental tally of what I had eaten so far that day: a bite of a fig Newton, a handful of pistachios and a couple bites from a Clif Bar. Not a lot but didn't think my stomach could take anything yet. Instead, I bought a Gatorade from the center and sat resting and sipping while I waited for Tami to arrive.

My right shoulder is nagging at me from the weird weight distribution of the pack when one side was wet and the other dry. Overall, I felt beat up, yet I will say that the Gatorade is helping me feel a bit better – that and being sheltered in a warm building.

Waiting in the center, I did a lot of thinking about my expectations of myself regarding the hike. I couldn't help wondering how I would have performed physically with younger bones, muscles and ligaments with no worries about making it back in time to secure a full-time job. Oh, and of course, also having less body fat to lug around. Unfortunately, I didn't know about any long-distance trails in my youth, let alone the Pacific Crest Trail.

Twenty minutes pass before I see Tami's car pull into the parking lot. I say goodbye to the volunteers and a few hikers I've chatted with, grab my pack from the porch and shuffle to the car. She is mad at me for wasting her weekend driving back and forth around southern California again. Sorry baby!

Epilogue

For two days after returning home, I was ill. I definitely picked up a bug from somewhere – even Tami got sick later. Before returning to work, I took an entire month to readjust to 'real life', or life off the trail. I used the time to start transposing my written journal and vlogs into this book and went on some fun outings with Tami to make up for the past two years of staying home and saving money for the hike. I used to dream a lot about the trail every night, but eventually that faded away.

I also was able to visit my parents a couple times over the summer. My father had been struggling with health over the past few years and by September (two months after I came off trail) the outlook was worse. By the end of the month he was gone. Just like that. If I was still on the trail, at that point I would be in Washington and perhaps close to finishing. As it is, I'm glad I was home and within a few hours of drive time to see him a couple times before the end.

All thru hikers say that the hike changes them. I did experience some of this even with hiking a mere 125 PCT miles, although some of the changes seem temporary. (Made to about mile 118 on trail and then slogged 7ish miles *back* to Warner Springs.) When I first came back, I was more patient and appreciative of other people, strangers and friends alike.

Normally a laid-back personality, I turn into a type A when behind the wheel – but for a short time after I returned from the trail I was not. (Sadly, I will admit that this particular change did not 'stick' as I'm back to saying a few choice words to the bad drivers out here during commute time.)

Some 'changes' that have stuck is my value over material things versus experiences. Yes, I still love my creature comforts, yet I see no need for 'things' that aren't useful. Sure, I still hold on to a few items that 'spark joy' but would rather own less useless items and have more money in the bank or instead spend that cash on journeys to experience new and amazing places alongside people I cherish.

Before setting off on this hike, I believed I was a tough old woman and still physically capable, not matter how overweight I'd gotten over the past decade or two. I truly believed my old athletic body would recover its youthful vigor and switch back into the way it was to power through the entire PCT. Well, part of that probably could be done with time, but what I hadn't considered was what the onset of arthritis does to one's body. At most, in everyday life, I'm a human barometer. When damp weather is coming, I feel it and sometimes have joints swell. Usually some Ibuprofen and movement takes care of that. Every day repeated overuse while hiking is a completely different story, plus I'm sure my weight contributed to the problems I began to experience. My 5'11" frame has always had some extra weight on it. While in my 20s, and younger, it was muscle weight with some fat – not a problem. Middle age has flipped that script though – now it's a problem. With time and effort, I will be able to go longer distances and carve out more sections of the trail, I'm just not sure that a thru-hike is a possibility. Section hiking *absolutely* is and I plan on conquering more sections in upcoming years. I learned that I'm not such a tough old bird after all.

Even though the hike only lasted 118 northbound miles of the PCT, it felt like a great adventure and I'm happy that I took the time to sufficiently record it in my written journal and vlog channel. Many details are already fading.

If I have any advice for aspiring thru hikers it is to do your research and hike, hike, hike. Watch vlogs, read books, ask questions – see what works for other hikers that have gone the distance. Keep this caveat in mind when collecting your data; what works for some may not always work for you – especially when it comes to gear. Test out whatever you purchase on at least overnight camp/hike excursions to see what works well and what doesn't and switch out the bad. Test everything! For example, many thru hikers use zero drop tennis shoes. I bought a pair and wore them to get used to the feel and although I loved the room I had in toe box, the flatness and nonsupport of those shoes left my feet in agony after only a few hours of wearing them. I found sturdy, but still breathable, hiking shoes with a decent sized toe box worked best for me. They may not for you, but you will never know until you hike around for hours in a pair yourself. Gear is personal, you must experience it to find the right fit for you.

***

What happened to the other hikers I met on my journey? I was able to follow up on most of the people I shared this adventure with.

Seraina from Switzerland nearly completed every mile of the trail – even making it through the Sierra. Talking with her after the hike, she said there were roughly 300 miles in Northern California she fell short of completing due to time constraints. Most people who enter the US to hike have specific entry visas that limit how many days/months you can stay. The clock is ticking once they enter the country.

I was unable to communicate with Arthur post trail but was able to tell from social media posts that he had completed the trail in just under six months. Job well done!

Freddy (Energizer) completed about 1100 miles and faced with the extra cost of flipping to different parts of the trail decided to keep his money in the bank and try to finish during another year.

Dutchman, AKA Erick, hiked until about mile 210 where the trail crosses under the I-10 freeway in Southern California near Cabazon and came off to help a family member. Later he was injured and was unable to continue.

Jessica, who I met crossing a stream the morning of the day we camped together at Fred Canyon finished a good chunk of the trail. The people she was hiking with skipped the Sierra and exited the trail for the season in mid Washington.

Hailing from the UK, Mary Mansfield (a popular YouTube vlogger) survived all sorts of curve balls the trail threw at her. She made it in one piece through the Sierra, albeit with a cracked rib, flipped up to Washington to knock out that state in decent weather, and returned to complete Oregon when winter was arriving in sleet and snow. If you ever get a chance to watch YouTube vlogs on hiking the PCT, hers is one you should watch. She completed the trail, not straight north to south, but finished it!

Mando hopped around a lot too and consistently was struggling with funds to finance the hike. It's not cheap to hike the trail – yes you live simply, and can live cheap and not in motels, but eventually need money for food and gear replacement. He flipped around and hiked different portions of the trail. I'm not sure how many miles, but he completed a fair amount and far more than me.

Sandal wearing Medicine Man reached the Sierra and made it to Mt. Whitney (a peak not directly on the PCT but close enough that a majority of hikers will attempt to summit), before having to back down and exit the high elevation because of health concerns. He spent 3 weeks down in elevation recovering and decided to flip north and begin a south bound, or SoBo hike, from Washington state. He was unable to complete it all but is looking forward to cleaning up the miles he hasn't set foot on yet.

Feet issues took out Chantel eventually a little past mile 210 where Erick exited the trail. Plantar Fasciitis is no joke. She rested in the Palm Springs area for a while to try again, but the feet just weren't cooperating.

Out of the four of us women who briefly got to hike with one another, Chris made it the farthest. (I'm not sure how far Betsy went on trail). Chris did some crazy amount of flipping around, hiking some of the trail south, some north and conquered the Sierra later in the season when the snow had melted, and the rivers were not raging any longer. The infamous weather window began to close in Washington though and conditions were becoming horribly sketchy. At Rainy Pass in Washington she decided to call it and go home. She had been out there for six months and her visa was also expiring. Oregon and part of Washington is still on her to-do list for a possible future hike on the PCT.

I was also friends with three couples that I had hoped to end up hiking with at some point while on trail, but it was not to be. Corey and Chelsea from Oregon made it into the Mission Creek 'mess' (see below) which is in the stretch of the trail between Whitewater Canyon and Big Bear in Southern California. Illness took them off trail coupled with money issues because of a sudden large veterinary expense back home. At least I was able to meet up with them in Idyllwild for lunch and a short visit while I was off trail.

Patti and Maru, who I camped with at Whitewater while testing out our gear months before had to split while on trail. I'm not sure where Maru exited, but Patti called it quits later after she reached Big Bear. The condition of the trail between Whitewater and Big Bear was bad because of flooding that February. Large portions of the trail were washed away, and hikers had to be creative cutting a new path and clambering up canyon walls. It took a lot out of some and after a rough time, Patti went home to recover.

I can't forget the dynamic duo from the UK, Heidi and Brian, the tough Liverpudlians. They also have great vlog documentation of their hike. Powering through, they entered the Sierra, but immediately started having issues with river crossings. Swollen rivers are one of the most dangerous things on trail. Forget the occasional black bear sighting, frequent rattlesnakes hiding along your path, even the rare cougar stalking you pales in comparison of crossing fast moving water. Heidi is a bit on the wee side of height, so water that may be knee high on a six-foot-tall hiker would be waist high on her... and waist high on a tall person up to her neck. I'm sure you understand the point. Not safe. Anyway, there were a couple of scary incidents that left them both jarred, and they exited the Sierra, flipped just north of them and continued onward. They kept pushing and in Washington, like others from outside the country, started seeing their visa date fast approaching. Someday they will come back and finish Washington and conquer the Sierra when the rivers are lower.

I will leave you with this quote from Bob Welch's *Cascade Summer: My adventure on Oregon's Pacific Crest Trail*:

> *Isn't the essence of adventure, be it big or small, the very idea that we might fail? Isn't it the tension that gives meaning to a story, the obstacles that steel us for the journey of life?*

The End… For Now.

Appendix
Gear, Gear and More Gear I Used

Backpack – ULA Catalyst

Footwear – For hiking: Keen Voyageurs, Smartwool socks. For camp: Oofos recovery flipflops.

Trekking Poles – Leki Cressidas

Tent – Big Agnes Copper Spur UL1

Sleep System – Gossamer Gear Thinlight pad, Big Agnes AXL Insulated air mattress, foil emergency blanket (underneath), Enlightened Equipment Revelation quilt, Trekology inflatable camp pillow.

Water Storage/Filtration – Smart Water bottles, CNOC 2L water bladder, Sawyer Mini Squeeze (later replaced with full sized Sawyer Squeeze).

Food System – JetBoil MicroMo, MSR Long Spoon, fuel cannister, ZPack large food bag, Opsak ziplock food bag.

Clothing – Patagonia Torrentshell Rain Jacket (which failed) replaced with Outdoor Research Helium Hybrid, Ghost Whisperer Puffy Jacket, Columbia Silver Ridge long sleeve shirt, Cuddle Duds thermal sleeping pants, a head buff, a balaclava, Outdoor Research Duo Tahoe/Volt short sleeve shirt, Columbia Convertible Hiking Pants/shorts, Exofficio 6" Boxer Briefs, Merino 150 Crew Long Sleeve pull over, 2 pairs of Darntough socks, Panama Jack hat, Dirty Girl Gaiters, Outdoor Research Sun Gloves, and Seirus Gloves for cold weather.

Toiletries – Travel sized toothbrush and toothpaste, toilet paper, ChapStick, hard shell case for my glasses, REI Snow Stake (doubles as a trowel and extra tent stake), antibacterial wipes, clippers, small hairbrush/mirror combo, Body Glide, sunblock, various medications/pills, small first aid kit which included Leukotape, Bandaids, tweezers and safety pins, and a small bottle of Wilderness Wash (I never did use this while hiking, but it came in handy for doing 'sink' laundry).

Emergency – Compass, whistle, lighter, duct tape, Leather Squirt PS4 multi tool, and small knife.

Electronics – Anker PowerCore 13000mAh, a small 10000mAh solar charger/power bank that died in Julian (replaced with an Anker 10000mAh), Anker quick charger with dual USBs, Petzl Bindi Headlamp 200 lumen, a small Gorilla pod, SticPik and other various camera/cell phone attachments, Samsung Galaxy S9+ (used to film and edit vlog), Garmin inReach Explorer GPS/Beacon/Satellite Phone, and various cords for charging.

Maps – Hard copies were from Halfmile – the versions that were once freely available to download and print from a PDF online. Electronic maps were from Guthooks application which was downloaded onto my phone and used satellite to triangulate position, much like a GPS would.

About The Author

L. Michele Scott was born in California in 1968 has been a disc jockey in radio, a writer, a teacher, a counselor, and information technology fix-it-gal among many other things. She holds two degrees from California State University at San Bernardino; a B.A. in History (2000) and a M.S. in Educational Counseling and Guidance (2006) and one from Riverside Community College in Computer Information Systems. As an avid geocacher and hiker, she has published articles in *FTF Geocacher; The Magazine For Geocachers*. She has also self-published fiction novels in different genres under L. Michele Scott and Leigh Ann Scott. Currently, she lives in Southern California with her partner, and three insane cats.

Connect Online

https://www.youtube.com/user/LMicheleS

https://www.instagram.com/geeky_girl_adventures/?hl=en

https://www.facebook.com/groups/1006435416220447

Printed in Dunstable, United Kingdom